Financial Starter Kit

Gain Financial Literacy and Avoid the Pitfalls of the American Dream

SYMONÉ B. "Beez"

XSCape
PUBLISHING
xscapepublishing.com

Our Company

In 2019, Adrian Kennedy began publishing books for independent authors from his office in Charlotte, North Carolina. His goal was to provide authors with more options and control over the publishing process at prices anyone could afford.

Today, the family owned and operated, Xscape Publishing company still continues to honor the founder's tradition of providing high-quality products and valuable services to the community.

First published by Xscape Publishing 2020

ISBN 978-1-7351852-1-7

Symoné B. "Beez" has no responsibility for the persistence or accuracy of URLs for external or third-party Internet Websites referred to in this publication and does not guarantee that any content on such Websites is, or will remain, accurate or appropriate. Designations used by companies to distinguish their products are often claimed as trademarks. All brand names and product names used in this book and on its cover are trade names, service marks, trademarks and registered trademarks of their respective owners. The publishers and the book are not associated with any product or vendor mentioned in this book.

None of the companies referenced within the book have endorsed the book.

Cover designed by using images from RawPixel.com

First edition

Contents

1

Introduction

We live in a world of instant gratification, and as a result, many of us have made our fair share of bad spending choices trying to appease our own sense of identity, or even worse, trying to keep up with the Joneses. Like many people, I had never taken a financial literacy course in my life. In which case, I wasn't familiar with how to pay bills or manage my money. I would later learn that I didn't know much, and man did it cost me. In making financial choices, I simply relied upon basic instincts. I later learned that financial literacy does not come with age; it is not like wisdom. It requires action, discipline, and sacrifice. My financial choices prior to this discovery would serve as the starting point for the direction of my future. Unfortunately for me, I started buried in debt in which I would have to eventually dig myself out. But I am here to tell you that this doesn't have to be your reality, and if it already is, your reality does not have to remain this way.

My Story

I had recently graduated, great job, good salary for an entry-level engineer. I was on top of the world, living the dream..... at least so I thought. It just so happened that my financial downfall came just as quickly as my ascension. My fall began with the purchase of my first home — new construction with all the bells and whistles. I had failed to do my research and educate myself on how much mortgage I could truly afford, and as a result, ended up purchasing a home that was too expensive. I wouldn't realize the severity of this decision until the transmission blew on my already paid-off car. Now I had a mortgage to pay and a car payment in addition to my credit card and student loan debt. I wasn't prepared at all. I was knee deep in debt and in a terrible spot both mentally and financially. However, I was able to make it out and find my way to financial freedom. The home I purchased is now a cash flowing rental property. I paid off my credit card debt in full. And I now own multiple businesses.

In this book, I hope to teach you the fundamental lessons that I learned in getting out of my terrible financial situation. This process will not be easy, but it will be rewarding and serve as your financial literacy starter kit that you can refer to at any time. If you follow the lessons in this book and remain dedicated, you can work your way to get out of debt and stay out of debt. You will also learn to change your spending habits and avoid what I call "financial traps".

* * *

Avoiding the Traps of the American Dream

Perhaps your idea of a successful life looks somewhat like this and in a somewhat similar order — graduate college, purchase a new car, invest in a big house, have an extravagant wedding with an extravagant honeymoon, then start a family. However, you will find that many who follow this path have not yet established a healthy financial foundation, and end up so deep in debt that they are living paycheck to paycheck while struggling to get ahead. In addition to this, they're most likely splurging on gifts, eating out, and going on vacations, keeping up with the latest trends, and upgrading cars every three to five years. You may be wondering how someone living paycheck to paycheck is able to afford this lifestyle. Most likely, they afford it by using credit cards and financing their lifestyle. Living far beyond their means and digging themselves into a deeper and deeper hole of debt.

You may think I am exaggerating about this being the common American lifestyle, but I'm not. Let's take a look at some statistics. According to Nerd Wallet, the American household owes an average of $6,849 in revolving

INTRODUCTION

credit card debt, $189,586 in mortgage debt, $27,804 in auto loans, and $46,822 in student loans.[1] Households are paying an average of $1,162 a year in credit card interest.[2] Ten percent of Americans say it will take them longer than 10 years to pay it off, and 9% don't think they will ever be able to completely pay off their debt.[3] With all of this debt racked up for the average American, you would assume that their incomes would be able to cover all of the expenses. Well, that simply isn't the case.

According to the U.S Bureau of Labor Statistics (BLS), the median income for a full-time worker was $46,800 before taxes.[4] This salary without savings in place is not a sustainable amount of money for retirement. In fact, only twenty-five percent of Americans have retirement savings.[5] Twenty-five percent! That's 3 in 4 people that have no plan for retirement. And please don't rely on social security being around. Additionally, the average American does not have enough money saved for an unexpected $400 expense.[6]

---

[1] Rathner, Sara.(2019). "NerdWallet's 2019 Household Debt Study." *NerdWallet*, https://www.nerdwallet.com/blog/average-credit-card-debt-household/.

[2] Rathner, Sara.(2019). "NerdWallet's 2019 Household Debt Study." *NerdWallet*, https://www.nerdwallet.com/blog/average-credit-card-debt-household/.

[3] Ten percent of Americans say it will take them longer than 10 years to pay it off, and 9% don't think they will ever be able to completely pay off their debt.

[4] TheStreet. (2020). *What Is the Average Income in the U.S. in 2019?*. [online] Available at: https://www.thestreet.com/personal-finance/average-income-in-us-14852178

[5] Harrison, D. (2020). *One-Quarter of Working Americans Have Zero Retirement Savings*. [online] WSJ. Available at: https://www.wsj.com/articles/american-households-remain-financially-fragile-fed-survey-shows-11558627721

[6] Bahney, A. (2018). *40% of Americans can't cover a $400 emergency expense*. [online] CNNMoney. Available at: https://money.cnn.com/2018/05/22/pf/emergency-expenses-household-finances/index.html

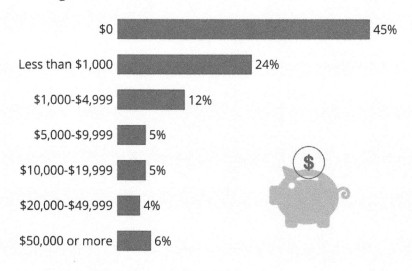

Most Americans Lack Savings

How much money do you have in your savings account?

$0	45%
Less than $1,000	24%
$1,000-$4,999	12%
$5,000-$9,999	5%
$10,000-$19,999	5%
$20,000-$49,999	4%
$50,000 or more	6%

n=846, survey conducted November 25-26, 2019
Source: GOBankingRates

The average net worth of a 35-year-old is only $11,100. When broken down by race, household wealth is declining for Black and Latino households. Shocking? It was for me. According to a study by Prosperity Now and the Institute for Policy Studies, the median wealth for Black Americans will fall to $0 by 2053 if current trends continue. Latino-Americans are also facing a decline in wealth which will hit $0 around the year 2073.

```
Net worth = Assets - Liabilities
```

The bottom line is that debt is a liability, so the more debt you have compared to assets, the lower your net worth will be.

INTRODUCTION

How much is your net worth? Don't be discouraged if you are in the negative. This just means you have some work to do.

Traps of the American Dream

We just determined that Americans are drowning in debt with no savings at all. However, if you take a look at social media, it would seem quite the opposite. It seems as though everyone has made it and is living like kings and queens. The reality is this: The middle class is being propped up by debt. Don't let the facades fool you, and don't fall for the traps shown below.

Trap #1 : Student Loan Debt

Trap #2 : Credit Card Debt

Trap #3 : Auto Loan Debt

Trap #4 : Mortgage Debt

Trap #5 : Wedding and Honeymoon Debt

Trap #6 : Vacation Debt

If you have fallen trap to any one of these, it isn't the end of the world. However, this means you need to get on track and stay on track to improve your financial situation. Now by indicating these traps, I am by no means eluding to discourage you from doing these things. I am simply saying there is a right way and a wrong way to go about paying for each of those things and avoiding the trap, which is living outside of your means. Should you not want to end up another American statistic, you should change the way you start thinking about debt and finances now.

Avoiding the Traps

To avoid these traps, you have to shift your mindset into not caring about what other people think. How many times have you made a financial decision based on the perception that it will give to others? I have done it before — we have all done it — but it will have to stop if you want to prosper. It is important to analyze your finances and make a note of the discretionary income that you have every month. Discretionary income is any income that you have leftover after your bills are paid. Yes, that means all bills from your rent or mortgage down to your …. It's important to track how you are spending your income. There are plenty of apps out there that make tracking your spending almost effortless. See if there are any expenses you can cut back on.

Here are some simple questions to ask yourself.

1. *What does most of my spending go towards? Entertainment, eating out, night life, subscriptions?*
2. *Am I overspending with credit cards and going into the negative every month?*

Like Ayesha Selden says, "Discretionary income is your net worth builder." If your discretionary income isn't being spent wisely, what means will you have to get ahead?

You will need to find ways to increase your income to create more discretionary income that can be used to pay down debt, save, or invest. Whichever route you choose, be disciplined and consistent with your plan. I find that it is easier to stick with a plan if you can find a friend or a group of people who want to revamp their finances and reach financial freedom as well. If you don't know anyone who would be open to this, consider looking for people who are doing Hugo's Stack Season. You should be able to find people by searching "Stack Season" on social media. Stack Season is a 13-week commitment to cutting back on all non-frivolous spending. It entails saving money, investing, paying off debt, and overall, just taking the time to improve yourself financially, physically, and spiritually.

INTRODUCTION

It will take some sacrifices for you to climb your way out of traps you have fallen into to reach financial freedom. These sacrifices are going to be temporary. It does not mean you need to cut back on your lifestyle for the rest of your life. A little sacrifice will go a long way, but you must also be disciplined as I mentioned earlier. You may only need to make a year or two of sacrificing to get to where you want to be, although some people may only sacrifice for a few months. The point is, a short period of sacrifices is worth a lifetime of financial freedom.

In summary, following these steps will help you avoid common financial traps and reach financial freedom.

Step 1: Change your mindset on spending and caring about what other people think about you.

Step 2: Cut back on discretionary spending

Step 3: Increase your income, pay down debt, and keep your lifestyle the same

Step 4: Improve your skillset, add more valuable skills, and surround yourself with like minded people

Step 5: Invest your discretionary money in assets that produce income

Step 6: Be consistent and disciplined with your financial plan

Step 7: Track your progress and make adjustments as needed

Remember that this is a process and nothing that is worth having comes overnight. As long as you stay consistent, work hard, and look for opportunities that align with your goals, you will succeed.

* * *

Financial Literacy Lingo

The focus of this section will be to teach you financial literacy terms you should become familiar with. After all, it is easy to be taken advantage of when you simply don't understand or are unfamiliar with what is being discussed. The terms listed below will serve as a starting point for common financial jargon you can expect to hear.

Definitions

- **Amortization Schedule** - A table of periodic loan payments showing the amount of principal and the amount of interest that makes up each monthly payment until the loan is paid off at the end of its term.
- **Annual Percentage Rate (APR)** - The yearly real cost of a loan including all interest and fees. The total amount of interest to be paid is based on the original amount loaned (aka principal), and is represented as a percentage.
- **Annual Percentage Yield (APY)** - APY, a commonly used acronym for annual percentage yield, is the rate earned on an investment in a year, taking into account the effects of compounding interest.
- **Appraisal** - A professional opinion of the market value of an asset.
- **Appreciation** - An increase in the value of an asset over time.
- **Asset** - Something that puts money in your pocket, such as real estate, stocks, app, website, etc.
- **Balance Sheet** - A financial statement that reports an individual's assets and liabilities at a specific point in time.
- **Balance Transfer** - Moving outstanding debt from one credit card to another card. Typically you will balance transfer to a card offering a lower interest rate, preferably 0% APR.
- **Balloon Loan** - A type of loan that does not fully amortize over its term. A balloon payment is required at the end of the term to repay the remaining principal balance of the loan.
- **Bankruptcy** - The legal proceeding involving a person or business that is unable to repay outstanding debts.

INTRODUCTION

- **Compound interest** - Interest that you earn on interest by reinvesting money.
- **Credit Limit** - The maximum amount of credit a financial institution extends to a client.
- **Debt Consolidation** - Combining more than one debt obligation into a new loan with a favorable term structure such as lower interest rate and lower monthly payment
- **Depreciation** - A reduction in the value of an asset that occurs over time as the asset gets older or as wear and tear occurs
- **Federal Student Loan** - A loan the federal government funds to help students or parents pay for the cost of a college education. To qualify for a federal loan, you will need to complete and submit a free application of student aid (FAFSA) form to the U.S. Department of Education.
- **FICO Score** - FICO score is a type of credit score created by the Fair Isaac Corporation. Lenders use borrowers' FICO scores along with other details on borrowers' credit reports to assess credit risk and determine whether to extend credit.
- **Guarantor** - A person who guarantees to pay a borrower's debt in the event the borrower defaults on a loan obligation.
- **Interest Rate** - The percentage of principal charged by the lender for the use of its money.
- **Liability** - Something that takes money out of your pocket.
- **Line of Credit** - An arranged amount of standing credit that a bank's customer may draw upon at any time.
- **Loan to Value (LTV) ratio** - A measure comparing the amount of your mortgage with the appraised value of the property.
- **Net Worth** - The value of all of your assets minus all of your liabilities. Net Worth = Assets - Liabilities
- **Personal Guarantee** - An individual's legal promise to repay credit issued to a business for which they serve as an executive or partner.
- **Principal** - The original sum of money borrowed in a loan or put into an investment

- **Private Student Loan** - A loan you can obtain from banks, credit unions or other lending institutions to help cover college expenses not met by scholarships, grants, federal loans, or other types of financial assistance.
- **Profit & Loss Statement** - A financial statement that summarizes the revenues, costs, and expenses incurred during a specified period, usually a fiscal quarter or year.
- **Refinance** - The process of taking out a new loan to pay off one or more outstanding loans.
- **Return on Investment (ROI)** - Measures how well an investment is doing.
- **Revolving Credit** - A type of credit that can be used repeatedly up to a certain limit as long as the account is open and payments are made on time.
- **Secured Loan** - A loan that has an asset, such as your home or car, pledged as collateral for the loan. If you default on the loan they will repossess the asset.
- **Tax Write Off** - Any legitimate expense that can be deducted from your taxable income on your tax return.
- **Term Loan** - A loan from a bank for a specific amount that has a specified repayment schedule and either a fixed or floating interest rate.
- **Unsecured Loan** - A loan that is issued and supported only by the borrower's creditworthiness, rather than by any type of collateral. Unsecured loans are approved without the use of property or other assets as collateral.

* * *

2

Creating a Solid Foundation

How to Gain the Most Value From This Book

I created this book to be an all-in-one financial literacy resource for you. A resource that you are able to revisit anytime you need some financial clarity. I want you to be able to gain the most value from the Financial Starter Kit by utilizing all of the free resources that I have made available to you.

1. Read this book and apply what you have learned in your everyday life.

2. Complete the Financial Starter Kit Checklist at the end of this book. If the Financial Starter Kit Checklist image in this book is too small for you, go to allocate.capitalsb.com to download the digital image.

3. Complete your money allocation spreadsheet then stick to your planned money allocation to create financial success. Download the free money allocation spreadsheet at allocate.capitalsb.com.

Bank Accounts

Bank accounts are an important aspect of financial literacy. Every year hundreds of millions of people pay fees to access their own money. Banking institutions are making a killing off of charging fees to their users in the form of monthly service fees, overdraft fees, and ATM fees. According to Bankrate here are some of the averages of fees financial institutions charge:

•   Overdraft fee: $33.36

- ATM fee: Close to $5
- Monthly service fee: checking accounts is $5.61 and about $15 for savings accounts
- Minimum amount required to open a checking account is $162.94 and about $575 for a savings account.[7]

I'm sure most people are very familiar with the ridiculous fees that banks charge you just to have an account. You don't want to be taken advantage of when it comes to banking fees, so this chapter will explain the different kinds of accounts, the difference between banks and credit unions, and which bank accounts I recommend you to sign up for to not fall victim to insanely high banking fees.

Banks vs Credit Unions

Banks are for profit institutions and credit unions are non-profit and customer owned. Credit unions have better customer service, lower fees, lower loan interest rates, and higher account interest rates. Banks have higher fees and lower account interest rates but are more convenient due to their nationwide network of banks.

Types of Bank Accounts

There are four types of bank accounts that you should be aware of and they all serve different purposes.

1. Checking Account
2. Savings Account
3. High Yield Savings Account
4. Money Market Account

---

[7] Dixon, A. (2019). *2019 Checking Account And ATM Fee Study | Bankrate.* [online] Bankrate. Available at: https://www.bankrate.com/banking/checking/checking-account-survey/

Checking Account

A checking account is a deposit account that allows an unlimited amount of transactions (deposits and withdrawals). These accounts usually come with a debit card and a checkbook. I recommend having a checking account for bills only. Do not withdraw from your bills checking account if it isn't bill related. I also recommend that people have a separate checking account for debit card expenses and everyday transactions such as gas, groceries, eating out, entertainment, etc.

Savings Account

A savings account is an interest-bearing non-transaction account that is limited to a maximum of six withdrawals per month due to Federal Reserve Board Regulation D. Most banks will either charge you a fee for the seventh withdrawal or decline all transactions over the limit of six withdrawals. If you exceed the maximum amount of six withdrawals too frequently some banks will close your account without notice, so make sure you are not exceeding the withdrawal limit.

High Yield Savings Account

A high yield savings account is typically an online savings account that offers higher interest rates compared to traditional savings accounts. A traditional savings account offers .001%-.10% APY depending on the amount of money that you keep in the account. High yield savings accounts offer around 0.5%-0.7% APY currently. This is more than 7x the amount of interest that you would earn from traditional savings accounts. *Note: High yield savings accounts rates are based on the federal interest rates. If the federal government lowers rates then high yield savings account rates will lower as well. If the federal government raises interest rates then high yield saving accounts rates will rise as well. COVID-19 has caused a decrease in rates.*

The nice thing about high yield savings accounts is that there is no minimum balance required to receive a higher interest rate. There isn't a high minimum amount required to open an account, usually no transfer fees, and you can open as many high yield savings accounts as you want to separate and allocate your money.

High yield savings accounts are a good place to stash your emergency fund and money that you are saving temporarily while you are figuring out where and how you want to invest your money. Keep in mind that since these accounts are online it typically takes 1 business day to transfer money out of your high yield savings account, but you shouldn't be withdrawing money often, so this shouldn't be a deal-breaker.

Recommended High Yield Savings Accounts

- Barclays Online Savings
- Ally Bank Online Savings
- Marcus (Goldman Sachs) Online Savings
- Discover Online Savings
- American Express High Yield Savings

High yield savings accounts are good for saving your money when you are building up your financial foundation and they are also good for saving 10% of your income. After you have built your foundation and created the discipline of saving, you will want to move from the act of saving to investing. A good foundation will consist of an emergency fund and having consumer credit card debt paid off.

Money Market Account

A money market account is very similar to a traditional savings account. The main difference is that they offer higher interest rates (nowhere near as high as high yield savings accounts), you have check-writing capabilities, and you are able to use a debit card. These accounts are still subject to the Federal Reserve Board Regulation D, meaning you are limited to a maximum of six transactions. Before high yield savings accounts were introduced, these were a good option for storing cash, but now they aren't as attractive.

Inflation

You may be wondering why you should care about what the interest rate is for your bank accounts. Inflation is why you should care. Inflation is the rate at which the price of goods and services increase over time. The inflation rate in the United States is around 3%, this means that $100 this year will only have the purchasing power of $97 next year and every year after that it loses an additional 3% of purchasing power. If you are the type that likes to save a lot of cash and not put your money to work, you are actually losing money every single year due to inflation. Remember, a dollar today is worth more than a dollar tomorrow due to inflation.

How many times have you seen something like, "Would you rather have $1,000,000 today or $2,500 a month for the rest of your life?". It would take 35 years for you to make a million dollars from the $2,500 option. Two-thousand and five-hundred dollars today will not seem like $2,500 in 10-15 years, so imagine how it will seem 35 years from now. In this scenario, personally, I'm always taking the cash now so I can invest it and put it to work.

Inflation is the reason why gas used to cost $0.80 in the 90s, but now costs $2.30-$3.00 depending on where you live. You know how people say $100 feels like $20 now? THAT is inflation. When you keep cash in accounts that do not earn interest, you are letting your money's purchasing power slowly dwindle away. If you are going to save money, you want to try to make as much interest on it as possible to try to keep up with inflation. Once you have established an emergency fund and have some extra money saved, you need to start putting your money to work through investments. Think of every dollar invested as a dollar working for you to make you more money.

Recommended Banks and Credit Unions

If you are tired of paying fees to your bank here are the banks and credit unions that I recommend.

Credit Unions

- Credit Unions Local to Your Area
- Digital Credit Union
- Navy Federal Credit Union (Military or DOD affiliation needed or referral)
- USAA (Military or DOD affiliation needed or referral)

Banks

- Ally
- Discover Bank
- Capital One 360 Checking

* * *

Solid Foundation

When it comes to creating a solid financial foundation you need to make sure that you have these four categories covered.

1. **Emergency Fund**
2. **Stocks**
3. **Real Estate or REITs**
4. **Life Insurance**

Emergency Fund

An Emergency Fund is a stash of money (preferably saved in a High Yield Savings Account) that has three months worth of expenses. You only tap into this emergency fund at times of emergency, as the name suggests. If you ever happen to fall on hard times, lose your job, have an unexpected large expense, etc. you will have a fund to tap into.

Three months worth of expenses should be the bare minimum. The more, the better. Think of each month of expenses saved as a month of freedom you have which will allow you to maneuver through life as you please. You won't have to stay at a job you hate or in a city you are just plain tired of. If you have the money available, you can give yourself the freedom to make changes when YOU want to make a change.

I suggest that people establish an Emergency Fund before looking to make investments outside of their 401(k). My reasoning behind this is that it is much harder to invest and KEEP money invested if you are investing the majority of the money that you have. Imagine you have $1000 saved and decide to use the entire $1000 to invest. The first few months things are going well, but suddenly you have an emergency and you have to pull out of your investment at a loss, or maybe you invested in something where you don't have access to the capital until 12 months of it being invested. Now you have to resort to either borrowing money from a friend or tapping into your credit card to pay for the emergency because you don't have any extra cash saved. You can avoid this entire scenario if you are patient and establish an emergency fund before you invest.

Remember, the path to wealth is a long game, so make sure that your foundation is solid. If you have no money saved, how can you get ahead? If you have no money saved, how can you pay for emergencies without ending up at square one again? You don't want every unexpected expense to set you back. Stack up, so these events don't affect you. Once you have an Emergency Fund and a little cushion it's time to focus on investing.

Stocks

When it comes to stock investing there are many ways to go about it. Investing in individual stocks, dividend stocks, Index Funds, Mutual Funds,

ETFs, and REITs are the different categories of stock investing. You can conduct research on all of these categories on Morningstar.com. Morningstar provides all of the information that you need to know about a stock before investing.

Individual stocks are shares of a company that you can purchase through a stock brokerage. When you purchase a share of a company's stock, you own a piece of the company. Dividend stocks are stocks that pay out dividends monthly or quarterly, so by holding the stocks, you are paid a dividend. Dividend stock investing is a good way to create passive income with very minimal work. When picking dividend stocks or dividend funds to invest in you want to look at their historical dividend payout performance. Some stock brokerages that you can look into to start investing are Robinhood, TD Ameritrade, and M1 Finance. These brokerages offer free trades and easy to use interfaces.

An Index Fund is a type of mutual fund. Index funds allow you to purchase a share of the fund and own the underlying assets in the fund. Index fund investing is an easy way to invest in stocks without worrying much and diversifying your portfolio. I consider that investing on autopilot because I prefer to invest in Index Funds that track the S&P 500. The S&P 500 Index or the Standard & Poor's 500 Index is a stock market index that tracks the stocks of 500 large-cap U.S. companies.

You might be wondering, why not just invest in the S&P 500? The answer to that is that the value of the S&P 500 is more than $3,000 per share, so it is out of reach for many people. If you invest in Index Funds that track the S&P 500, you can expect to see an average return of 7% per year long-term. My favorite Index Fund that tracks the S&P 500 is Vanguard's Total Stock Market Index Fund (VTSAX). I like this fund because the expenses are very low, and it has a proven track record with a long history. You can purchase shares of this index by opening an account with Vanguard.

An Exchange Traded Fund (ETF) is a basket of securities, stocks, bonds, commodities, or some combination of these. An ETF is similar to a mutual fund, but the difference is that you do not own the underlying assets when purchasing an ETF as you do with a mutual fund and Index Fund.

Real Estate or REITs

Real Estate is one of the oldest forms of wealth building. Eighty percent of millionaires own real estate. By building up a rental portfolio of single family homes, multifamily homes, or mobile homes you are able to generate passive income from the cash flow of your properties. Cash flow is your net profit after all expenses are paid on a rental property. When calculating the cash flow of a property, you want to take into account the cost of the mortgage, maintenance, property management cost, and any other expenses that may come along with the property. When you focus on cash flow with rental properties you can use the income to reach financial freedom. You can house hack to get an easier start to real estate investing and easily add units to your portfolio as well.

Maybe you aren't interested in owning any physical real estate at all, but still want to have exposure to the real estate market. Real estate investment trusts (REITs) are a perfect option for you. REITs are investment funds that purchase real estate all across the nation and provide dividend based income and total returns to their investors. Historically, REITs have grown at an average of 12.99% a year on average. You can purchase shares of REITs from stock brokerage websites such as Fidelity, Vanguard, TD Ameritrade, or Charles Schwab.

Life Insurance

Life insurance is important so you have money that is passed down to your family after your death. Life insurance is extremely cheap and there is no reason not to be signed up for a policy. Having peace of mind that your family will be okay after you pass away is a good feeling. You do not want to burden your family with financial stress after passing away. There are two types of life insurance: term life insurance and permanent life insurance. Term life insurance is for a specific period of time that pays out a death benefit and has no cash value that you can withdraw from. Once your term life policy has ended, you have to buy another policy at an older age and higher costs.

Permanent life insurance provides death benefit coverage for the life of the insured. Index Universal Life (IUL) life insurance is a type of permanent insurance that is more expensive because it has a cash value that can be withdrawn from. The cash in these IUL policies grow tax-deferred, and the cash accumulation is tied to the performance on an index. You are also able to take loans from the cash value of these policies. Do your due diligence before choosing a permanent life insurance plan.

* * *

The 'B' Word

I'm sure everyone has heard of the word "budgeting". We aren't going to use that word in this book. I don't know what it is, but people hate the word "BUDGET". The word "budget" is always met with high resistance and disdain. From now on I want you to view "budgeting" as "money allocation". When you receive money you aren't going to "budget the money" you will "allocate the money" into its respective bank account for a specific purpose. Looking at your income as money that needs to be allocated gives you a different perspective of money. It allows you to look at money in a non-restrictive way.

Every single dollar that you earn should be allocated in a manner that most benefits you. Don't get what I am saying confused with thinking that every single dollar you earn needs to be invested. I am saying that you need to have a plan for your money before it is received to maximize its value. I am going to teach you how to allocate your money in a way that allows you to not have to worry about thinking about how to divide your money once you are paid, not have to worry about if you have enough money for bills, or if you are meeting your savings goals for the month.

CREATING A SOLID FOUNDATION

This section will teach you how to use my Money Allocation spreadsheet. Remember, you can download this spreadsheet for free at allocate.capitalsb.com.

Bank Account Structure

The way that your bank accounts are structured is a vital key to the success of your money allocation. You want to make sure that you have multiple bank accounts that are for a specific purpose to separate your money. I have noticed that many people only have two bank accounts, one checking and one savings account. When they get paid pretty much all of their money goes into the one checking account. All expenses such as bills, gas, groceries, everyday spending, and entertainment are taken from this one account and whatever is leftover, if any, gets transferred into the savings account at the end of the month. Below is an image showing how most people manage their money and another image showing how you should be managing your money.

Incorrect money management

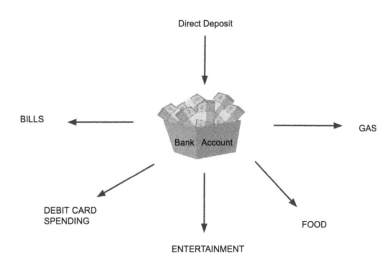

Correct money management

Direct Deposit

| BILLS | DEBIT CARD EVERYDAY SPENDING | DISCRETIONARY SPENDING | High Yield Savings |

CREATING A SOLID FOUNDATION

<u>Minimum Allocation Structure</u>

2 Checking Accounts

1 Savings Account

1 High Yield Savings Account

<u>Preferred Allocation Structure</u>

3 Checking Accounts - Bills, Everyday Spending, and Entertainment

1 Savings Account - Cushion Money

2 High Yield Savings Accounts - Emergency Fund and Investment

How to Determine Your Allocations

To determine how you want to allocate your money you must first look at your total income and expenses from the previous month. You can use a financial application called Mint (Mint.com) to get an accurate picture of your expenses or you can download your bank statements to manually evaluate your expenses. Let's say you don't use Mint and would like to run the numbers manually. It is good to write down with a pen and paper to take a real look at your finances. We will be creating your allocations based on your monthly totals.

You will have 3 sections.

INCOME, EXPENSES and SAVINGS/INVESTMENTS

FINANCIAL STARTER KIT

INCOME

1. Gather your pay stubs from last month and add up your NET pay from each paycheck. This will be your **total monthly job income**.
2. If you have a business or a side hustle that you earn an income from. Calculate the total amount of profit that you made last month. This will be your **total monthly business/side income**.
3. If you have any investment income, calculate the profit that you made last month. This will be your **total monthly investment income**.

EXPENSES

1. Gather all of your bills from the previous month by looking at your bank account statement and highlighting all of the bills (Rent/Mortgage, Utilities, Car Payment, Car Insurance, Student Loans, Personal Loans, Insurance, Streaming Services, Gym Memberships, etc). This will be your **total monthly bills.**
2. Gather your credit card statements from the previous month, and calculate the total amount of monthly minimum payments. This will be your **total monthly credit card payments.**
3. Gather your bank statements from the previous month and calculate the total amount spent on gas, groceries, and transportation expenses. This will be your **total monthly everyday spending**. *Note: Keep track of each of these categories separately and only keep track of the necessary spending.*
4. All remaining expenses will be categorized as **discretionary spending** (eating out, self care, entertainment, etc.)

SAVINGS/INVESTMENTS

1. Calculate the total amount of money that you saved or invested from the previous month. This will be your **total monthly savings/investments.**

An example of what your financial spending overview would look like when done by hand is shown below.

Financial Spending Overview

INCOME
>   Work =
>   Freelance =
>   Bonus =
>   Business =

EXPENSES
>   Rent / Mortgage =
>   Utilities =
>   Car Payment =
>   Car Insurance =
>   Student Loans =
>   Personal Loans =
>   Credit Card Min Payments =
>   Gym Membership =
>   Streaming Services =
>   Everyday Spending =

>   -------------------------------
>   Discretionary Income Left Over

SAVINGS/INVESTMENTS
>   Savings =
>   Investments =

>   Discretionary Income - Savings - Investments = Remaining Spending/Play Money

Source : Capital SB . BookWithBeez.com

Once you have a clear picture of your finances you can determine how you want to allocate your money. Take this time to make a note of any spending that you can cut back on. For example, monthly subscriptions that you aren't using, entertainment, too much discretionary spending, etc.

Paying Yourself First

Most people focus on paying everyone else first then spending whatever remains, which looks like this. **INCOME - EXPENSES = Remaining Amount Left to Spend**

You get paid, then shell out money for your bills, then you spend whatever is left over to enjoy life, then at the end of the month any money that may be left is saved. A lot of the time there is usually no money left to save, so you tell yourself "Next month I will do better to save." I know I've been there, I used to live the same way until I read The Richest Man in Babylon by George S. Clason and changed my mindset.

I recommend you to pay yourself FIRST every single time you get paid. Paying yourself first means to take a percentage of everything that you make and save it. If you can, take 10% of your monthly income and save it in an emergency fund. This will ensure that you will always stay ahead and save a portion of your earned income. This is what it looks like to pay yourself first.

INCOME - 10% of INCOME - EXPENSES = Remaining Amount Left to Spend

I want you to think about how much money you would have stashed away if you paid yourself 10% of all of your income since you started working. The number is staggering, and probably more than what you have in savings now. Then think about all of the money you spent on things you didn't need or don't have anymore. I encourage you to try paying yourself first from now and letting me know how it works out for you.

How to Allocate on Autopilot

Set up direct deposit through your company's payroll website and allocate your savings, bills, everyday spending, and discretionary spending to their respective accounts as shown in the "Bank Account Structure" section earlier in this chapter.

When you are setting up your direct deposit amounts make sure that you are taking your total monthly amounts and multiplying by 12 to get the yearly total. Then you need to divide by the number of times you get paid a year. If you are paid biweekly, divide the yearly amount by 26. If you are paid twice a month divide the yearly amount by 24.

How to Set Up Direct Deposit Amounts

<u>Paid Biweekly</u>

(Monthly total x 12) / 26 = direct deposit allocation amount

<u>Paid Twice a month</u>

(Monthly total x 12) / 24 = direct deposit allocation amount

Most companies allow you to disburse your paycheck into six or more bank accounts. Take advantage of the automatic money allocation that your company allows. This will help you not have to think about how you need to allocate your money every time you get paid. You won't have to worry about having enough money to pay the bills. It cuts down on monthly transfers and saves you time.

Below is an example showing how you can allocate your money through your company's payroll system.

Direct Deposit Details							
Account Type	Transit Number		Account Number	Deposit Type	Amount or Percent	Deposit Order	Edit	Remove
Checking	074000010	****56		Amount	$500.00	2	🖉	🗑
Savings	074000010	******66		Percent	10.00%	3	🖉	🗑
Checking	074000010	******67		Balance of Net Pay		999	🖉	

Add Account

Contact your payroll to find out if your company allows multiple bank accounts for direct deposit.

How to Allocate for the Known Unexpected Expenses

When you are making your allocations you have to think about what I call the "Known Unexpected Expenses". These known unexpected expenses consist of car maintenance, birthday gifts, anniversary gifts, holiday gifts, basically any expenses that you pay yearly no matter what. Many people never set money aside for car maintenance and when something unexpected happens to their car they struggle to pay the expense. I consider car maintenance a known unexpected because you know that you have to maintain your car whether it is an oil change, tire replacement, window/windshield replacement, battery, etc. I recommend setting aside a minimum of $20 per paycheck into a maintenance fund (can be a bank account or save cash in an envelope). If you save $20 per paycheck you will set aside $480-$520 a year for car maintenance.

Note: You should adjust this based on the past maintenance costs for your vehicle.

For gifts, you want to look at how much money you spend a year on gifts and set aside money each paycheck for your gift fund. Deposit your gift fund into a gift fund bank account or save the cash in an envelope. High yield savings accounts are free, so I find them to be an easy way to save money for these expenses. The Known Unexpected Expenses fund method can be applied to any expected expense that you may have.

* * *

Financial Scoreboard

Assets vs Liabilities

Assets and liabilities are what make up your financial progress. The more income producing assets you acquire the more money you have coming in monthly for financial freedom. An asset is something that puts money in your pocket. A liability is something that takes money from your pocket.

People have different opinions on what is considered an asset and what is a liability. Personally, I do not look at cars and primary homes as assets on my net worth, because they do not generate income for me on a monthly basis or in the near term. Cars and homes typically take money from you every single month in the form of maintenance and monthly payment. Some may argue that their home is gaining equity, but if you aren't planning to sell, you are not capturing any of the equity. And, if you did decide to tap into the equity without selling, it can only be done in the form of a loan called a Home Equity Line of Credit (HELOC).

There are exceptions to primary homes and cars generating income. If you use your home to house hack then it is putting money into your pocket every month. If you use your car to Uber, Lyft, or Door Dash your car is also putting money into your pocket every month, but for most people, this is not the case. You are entitled to calculate your net worth however you may please and it is your personal preference on how you view primary homes and cars. This is personal finance, so you control your ideologies and methodologies.

Types of assets

- Retirement Accounts (401Ks, IRAs, etc.)
- Checking and Savings Accounts
- Current value of any real estate that you own
- Investment Accounts (Stocks, Options, 529 Plans, etc.)

Types of Liabilities

- Real estate mortgages
- All loans (Home Equity Loans, Car Loans, Student Loans, Personal Loans, etc.)
- Credit Card Balances
- Unpaid Outstanding Bills (Hospital Bills, Property Taxes, etc.)

Net Worth

Net Worth is like a scoreboard for tracking your financial progress in life. Net worth is the net value of the things that you own. The higher the score, the better you are doing. The lower the score the worse you are doing. If the score is negative, you are heading in the wrong direction in your financial journey.

FINANCIAL STARTER KIT

```
To calculate Net worth,
Net worth = Assets (what you own) - Liabilities (what y
ou owe)
```

When you decide to take your net worth seriously you should first take a look at what your net worth currently is; perform a benchmark assessment of where you should be, then perform the assessment again with a future age as a short term (1- 5 year) goal to reach.

A benchmark that I like to use and is standard in personal finance is,

```
Net worth target = (Age x Pre-Tax Income) / 10
```

If you want to see what your net worth should be at a future age, you would change your age accordingly. If you have a good idea of what your future income would be you would change the pre-tax income value as well. I believe that this formula only works well up to about age 40.

A good number to aim for a long-term net worth, and that depends on your personal goals for the most part. Some people may want a $500,000 net worth, some may want $10,000,000 net worth, some may want a $1,000,000 net worth, and some may want a billion-dollar net worth. It all comes down to your personal goals. Below is a graph of the average net worth for the above-average person.

THE AVERAGE NET WORTH OF THE ABOVE AVERAGE PERSON					
Age	Years Worked	Avg. Pre-Tax Savings	Avg. Post-Tax Savings	Avg. Property Equity	Avg. Total Net Worth
22	0	$0	$0	$0	$0
23	1	$12,750	$7,500	$0	$20,250
24	2	$31,750	$15,000	$0	$46,750
25	3	$54,000	$25,000	$0	$79,000
30	8	$165,000	$67,500	$17,500	$250,000
35	13	$284,000	$115,000	$30,000	$429,000
40	18	$427,750	$162,500	$70,000	$660,250
45	23	$596,500	$200,000	$117,500	$914,000
50	28	$840,250	$237,500	$162,500	$1,240,250
55	33	$1,184,000	$275,000	$225,000	$1,684,000
60	38	$1,577,750	$312,500	$290,000	$2,180,250
65	43	$2,121,500	$375,000	$375,000	$2,871,500
Source: FinancialSamurai.com					

You should perform financial check ups on your net worth at least twice a year to make sure that you are on track with your financial plan. You can perform the check-ups on Personal Capital (Use my link pc.capitalsb.com

30

and get a free $20) and viewing your net worth, cash accounts, debt, and liabilities.

The more assets you acquire compared to your liabilities the higher your net worth will be. You can accelerate your net worth and monthly income goals by investing at a higher savings rate, investing in cash flowing real estate, creating a business, and owning digital assets.

* * *

3

Making Credit Work For You

What is Credit and How to Build It Without Going into Debt

Growing up, I was always told that credit was bad and that it was something that I should mostly stay away from to avoid ending up in massive credit card debt. I was never taught about the benefits of good credit, how to responsibly use credit, and how to build my credit. Credit, when used responsibly, will make your life much easier. Nowadays without good credit, it is a hassle to open an account with a utility company or a cell phone bill. Credit is required to obtain most of the basic necessities (i.e. apartment, utilities, non-prepaid cell phone, car, and mortgage). The less you have to stress about these things the better.

Credit Report

Starting out, you want to know what is on your credit report. You can access your credit report from all three credit bureaus— Experian, Equifax, and TransUnion—for free on AnnualCreditReport.com once a year. These reports will not have your FICO score, the report is used for ensuring that all of the information on your credit file is accurate and up to date. It is good practice to save a copy of these credit reports in a safe place. If you want to obtain your FICO score, but you don't have any credit cards or financial institutions that provide a FICO score for free, you can purchase your scores on MyFico.com. They offer one report from one bureau for $19.95 or reports from all three bureaus for $59.85. All of their reports include FICO score, mortgage score, auto score, and credit card scores.

There are different FICO scoring models used for mortgages, auto loans, and credit cards, so it is good to know where you stand for each type. They also offer monthly monitoring. I took advantage of their monthly credit monitoring package while I was going through my mortgage underwriting process. The last thing you want to happen while going through the mortgage process is for something to lower your score unexpectedly.

A free credit monitoring option that I like to use is Credit Karma. Yes, I said creditkarma.com is one of my go tos. I like using Credit Karma for monitoring my credit report. I do not advise using Credit Karma for scoring because their scores aren't accurate so DO NOT use Credit Karma for your credit score. They immediately notify you of new inquiries, late payments, and bills that have gone to collections. Now that you know how to pull your credit report, view your real FICO credit score, and monitor your credit, we will discuss the key factors that make up a FICO credit score.

Key FICO Credit Scoring Factors

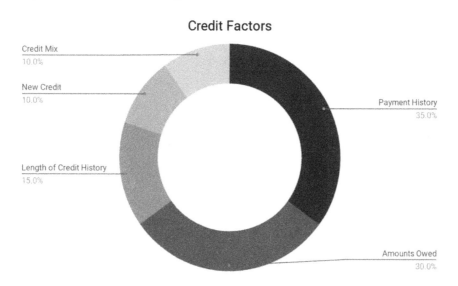

- Payment History - 35%
- Amounts Owed - 30%

- Length of Credit History - 15%
- New Credit - 10%
- Credit Mix - 10%

Payment History

Payment history has the greatest effect on your score and is the most important because collections stay on your credit score for seven years (unless you can get it removed early via a dispute). *Note: Paying off a collections bill does not mean it will be removed from your credit report. Therefore it will still negatively impact your score. A full removal is the only way for a collection to stop impacting your score before 7 years have passed.*

Late payments 30/60/90 days also stay on your report for seven years. Late payments after 30 days of being late are reported to credit bureaus. After a long period of non-payment the bill will be sent to a collection agency. Having a bill go to collections can make your score drop 50 to 100 points and will continue to hurt your score for seven years until it is removed from your credit report. It is extremely important to stay on top of bills and make sure they never go to collections. The KEY factor to a high score is having 0 bills in collections. It is very hard to obtain a score in the 700s if you have bills in collection. The next major factor is credit utilization.

Amounts Owed

Credit card utilization is the balance that you are carrying on a credit card compared to your credit card limit.

```
To calculate credit utilization,
Credit Utilization =
(Total credit card balance / Total credit card limit) x 100
```

Overall credit utilization is the total balance across all cards compared to the total credit limits across all cards.

```
To calculate overall credit utilization,
Overall Credit Utilization = ( Total credit card balances / T
otal credit card limits ) x 100
```

Example 3.1:

Let's say you have three credit cards with a $1,000 limit on each for a total of $3,000. You owe $500 on one credit card with a $1,000 limit.

The utilization on that credit card is 50%. ($500 / $1,000) x 100 = 50%.

Your total overall credit utilization would be 17% ($500/$3,000 x 100) = 17%.

To calculate your utilization take your total balance and divide it by the total credit limit, do this for each credit card that you have. To calculate your total overall credit utilization take your total balances across all credit cards and divide it by the total credit limits across all credit cards.

For the best scores possible, it is recommended that your total overall credit utilization is no higher than 30%. Having a credit utilization less than 10% on ONLY ONE card and all other cards reporting a $0 balance. This is called the All Zero Except One method. This can be overkill for a lot of people, so the main take away here is to keep balances low and don't carry monthly balances. You don't want to be paying interest and carrying credit card debt anyway. You should be paying off everything in full each month. Zero dollars in credit card debt should be the goal.

Length of Credit History

Length of credit history is the TIME factor that many people try to bypass. You cannot cheat time, so you have to be patient here and just wait for the length of your credit history to mature. Don't expect to have a score in the 700s if you have less than 4 years of credit history.

New Credit

Opening new accounts too often will also lower your average age of accounts and every new hard credit pull is a new inquiry. The average age of accounts (AAoA) is how old your average loan/credit card is. Adding new credit cards and loans lowers your AAoA.

A hard pull is when a lender pulls your credit report and it is reported to the bureaus that it was pulled. You can expect a hard pull to be reported to your credit report when applying for a mortgage loan, auto loan, a credit card, and starting utility services. A soft pull is when it is not reported. ALWAYS ask if it will be a hard pull or soft pull before a lender runs your credit. Credit inquiries stay on your account for two years but stop hurting your score after one year. It is best to keep the total number of inquiries no more than five inquiries per 24 months.

Credit Mix

The last factor is your credit mix. Do you have credit cards, car loans, mortgage, student loans, or secured loans? If so, you need a good mix of secured and unsecured loans for the best credit score results. Remember, a good credit mix only accounts for 10% of your score, so it is not needed to get a score in the 700s. I was able to reach a score of 720 with only a secured credit card.

Excellent Credit Does Not Equal High Loan Amounts

It is a common misconception that an 800 credit score means you will get approved for any loan amount that you can think of. How many times have you seen "Would you take an 800 credit score or $100,000 cash? " on social media? I see so many people chose the credit score over the money. If you want a higher credit score because you have bad marks on your credit report, you can repair it yourself for free or hire a credit repair professional. Choosing an 800 credit score as opposed to $100,000 cash shows that most people don't understand how credit works. Perhaps prior to reading this book, you thought an 800 credit score would be better. Let me convince you otherwise by teaching you how credit works.

The two major factors in determining your loan approval amount are

1. Income
2. Amount of debt

These two factors make what is called your debt to income (DTI) ratio. Your debt to income ratio is used to determine how much debt you can afford. You can have an 800 credit score, but a low income and not be approved for many loans because the lenders will see that you cannot afford to service the debt. Your DTI ratio is all of your monthly debt payments divided by your gross monthly income.

```
To calculate your DTI ratio,
Debt to Income =
( Total Monthly Debt Payments / Gross Monthly Income ) x 100
```

Example 3.2 :

You make $2,000 a month and you pay a $150 student loan payment, $200 car payment, and $50 worth of minimum credit card payments. Your total monthly debt payments are $400. ($400 / $2,000) x 100 = 20% DTI ratio. To calculate your DTI ratio divide your monthly payment amounts by your gross monthly income.

A 43% DTI ratio is usually the maximum for mortgage lenders to approve you for a mortgage. However, some lenders will still approve you if you have more than a 43% DTI ratio. I recommend that people keep their DTI as low as possible because you don't want to spend a large amount of your income on debt and monthly payments. The higher your total amount of monthly payments are, the less discretionary income you have available to save and invest. Keeping your monthly payments low is key to financial freedom!

* * *

How to Build Credit

Step 1: Secure your first credit card

I'm sure everyone has heard the myth, "You have to go into debt to build credit!". This couldn't be further from the truth. You can start building credit by getting a secured credit card, and you should be paying your balance off in FULL every month to not pay interest. A secured credit card requires you to deposit cash to establish a credit limit. For example, if you get approved for a $250 secured credit card you will need to deposit $250. This way you aren't going into debt because you are spending from the $250 that you deposited. I recommend Discover because they allow you to graduate from a secured credit card to an unsecured credit card. With an unsecured credit card you don't have to deposit any money to establish a credit limit.

I believe that the Discover IT is one of the best credit cards to have in your wallet due to the free FICO scoring, 5% rotating categories, free social security number monitoring, and 0% - 4.99% APR Balance Transfers. I used a secured credit card to build my credit and my first unsecured credit card was the Discover IT; I still love it to this day. You can apply for this card at the end of the book in the 'Resources' section.

To avoid paying interest and going into debt, you should be paying off your credit cards in FULL every single month. This requires discipline and not spending more than you can afford. At the bare minimum, you should set your credit cards up to auto pay for the minimum balance so you will never receive a late payment or pay any late fees.

A simple way to keep your credit card spending under control is to only use it for gas and groceries. Your everyday spending allocation should already be established so you will be able to easily pay off your credit card every month with no issues. Now, some people may be thinking, "Wait I thought people recommend you to put all of your spending on your credit card to maximize points." This is true, some people recommend this but if you aren't disciplined and don't pay your balance off in full every month, you will not see real benefits from the points. By overspending and not paying your balance off in full, the interest will cancel out pretty much any benefits you thought you were getting from points.

Once you gain the discipline to make all of your purchases on the credit card, do so, but as soon as you start to overspend you need to revert back to gas and grocery spending only. After 8 to 12 months of responsible spending on your first credit card, your score should have increased due to your credit history reporting to the credit bureaus. Take advantage of the free FICO score from Discover to track your credit score.

Step 2: Apply for 2-3 More Credit Cards

Step 3: Don't Miss Any Payments or Let Anything Go Into Collections

Step 4: Be Patient and Wait

Building and maintaining an excellent credit score is simple when you focus on the five factors below.

1.   Time
2.   Low credit utilization
3.   NO delinquencies (late payments or collections)
4.   NEVER miss a payment & ALWAYS pay on time
5.   Don't open too many cards/get too many hard pulls in a short period of time (within 12 months)

Types of Credit Cards

Annual Fee

Annual Fee (AF) credit cards charge you annually for having the credit card. Typically these cards offer benefits for its credit cardholders to offset the AF. Do not sign up for AF cards if you are not going to be able to maximize the card's benefits. For example, if you don't travel, do not sign up for a travel credit card with an AF. Opt for a similar credit card that does not have an annual fee if you will not be able to maximize the value. Another rule of thumb is to not sign up for cashback credit cards that have annual fees.

Travel Credit cards

Travel credit cards give you points for spending on travel expenses such as hotels, airline tickets/fees, and rental cars. Travel credit cards allow people to maximize the value from their travel spending to redeem points for additional points or cash. You usually get more value by using the points to travel, but don't feel bad for choosing the cash option instead.

<u>Cashback Credit Cards</u>

Cashback credit cards give you a percentage of cashback based on your credit card spending. Most cashback cards offer between 1% - 5% of cashback rewards. With these cards, you don't want to spend on items you wouldn't typically purchase for the sake of earning cashback. Remember 1% cashback on $1,000 is only $10, so don't go into debt trying to chase cashback rewards. If you don't pay your balance off in full, the interest paid will cancel out the cashback reward that you earned.

What You Shouldn't Do With Credit

You should not cosign on anyone else's loans, leases, etc. Cosigning is when you add yourself as a guarantor on someone else's loan payments or monthly apartment lease payments. Being a guarantor means that you are guaranteeing to help make the payments if the borrower cannot afford to do so. You will be putting your credit at risk if the person that you cosigned for does not pay their bills on time. If they stop paying their bills the debt will be sent to collections and it will ruin your credit. Think long and hard about cosigning for anyone, family included.

You shouldn't add anyone as an additional cardholder on your credit card who isn't family. Adding someone as an additional cardholder is when you allow someone else access to your credit card. They will receive their own card but will be tied to your credit limit. If the person that you add spends money on the credit card and they can't afford to pay it back you are on the hook for paying down their credit card.

The last thing that you should not do with credit is act like it is a free unlimited source of money. Credit card interest is how the credit card companies make money and if you are paying credit card interest, you are not using your credit cards responsibly. Do not spend more than you can afford to pay back in the same month if you want to stay out of credit card debt.

* * *

Auto Loans

When shopping for auto loans, in most cases, you should go into the dealership already pre-approved for financing from an outside credit union or bank. The only time this wouldn't apply is if you are trying to get a 0% APR loan that the dealership is offering. In most cases, you want to walk into the dealership with a check from your bank.

What to Look for When Obtaining an Auto Loan

How many times have you heard people say to just focus on the monthly car payment when buying a car? As long as you can "afford" the monthly payment you are fine, right? WRONG. When financing a car, you want to focus on four main factors. **Do not move forward** with anything until you write down and understand these factors of the loan you are applying for and are about to accept.

1. Interest Rate (APR)
2. Length of the Loan
3. Monthly Payment Amount
4. Total Cost of the Loan

Interest Rate (APR)

The annual percentage rate (APR) on a car loan is the annual cost you will pay to finance a vehicle. You should be aiming to obtain the lowest interest rate for your auto loan. At the time of writing this book, auto loan interest rates are between 2.49% - 6.29%. To determine the current average for an auto loan interest rate, you should Google "current auto loan rates" and click on Bankrate's website to view the average interest rates. Some dealerships offer 0% APR to people with excellent credit, so if you can take advantage of this rate and you want to finance, do so. A 0% loan is borrowing money for free, but know that it may be harder to get a good deal on a car if you want a 0% loan and they are only available for new cars.

Length of the Loan

The length of an auto loan is typically 36 months (3 years), 48 months (4 years), 60 months (5 years), 72 months (6 years), and 84 months (8 years). I don't recommend anyone to get an auto loan over 60 months. If you are unable to get approved for a 60-month loan, chances are you cannot afford the car you are trying to buy. Dealerships will try to extend the length of the loan to get your monthly payment to an amount that you have determined you can afford. The longer the length of your loan, the more interest you will pay. Remember, the total cost of the loan that is being financed is an important factor. Always pay attention to how much interest you will pay over the life of the loan. You can save yourself money by making additional payments to the principal of the loan to pay off your auto loan early.

Monthly Payment Amount

Your monthly payment amount is important because you need to be able to afford your car payment. I suggest that you calculate how much you can afford to spend on a car by looking at your finances (income - expenses). After determining how much you are able to spend, run the numbers in an auto loan calculator. I suggest that you use Calculator.net Auto Loan Calculator to run the numbers. I like this calculator because you can see the total price of the loan, and you can put in the monthly payment that you are aiming for as well as the length of the loan, interest rate, and down payment amount to determine what the max price is of the car that you can purchase.

Total Cost of the Loan

The total cost of the loan consists of the vehicle price, total interest, taxes, and fees. Pay attention to the cost of the vehicle compared to the total cost of the loan. High interest rates will add thousands to the total cost of the loan. Don't be afraid to ask, "What is the total amount of interest over the life of the loan?".

How to Get an Auto Loan Approval

You want to "shop around" to find the lowest interest rate for auto loans. This means looking at the banks/credit unions that you already have an account with and applying for 2-3 loans at different banks/credit unions. Typically, a credit score over 740 will get you the lowest rate (best rate), a credit score of at least 675 will give you a good rate (average rate), and a credit score lower than 650 will get you a high rate (worst rate). When applying for loans, make sure to do so within a 30 day period so that only one inquiry will be counted against your credit score. The credit bureaus will see that you were pricing out the best loan option. If you spread out the applications for these loans, however, multiple inquiries will be counted against your credit score.

When shopping around for auto loans you want to make sure that you are comparing the correct loan rates based on the car you want to finance. You will receive different rates based on the age of the car and the total amount of the loan. Make sure you are comparing similar rates when shopping for an auto loan. Below I have shown an example of new car loan rates compared to used car loan rates.

Note: N/A means that they do not offer loans for that term length based on the loan type.

New & Used Car Loan Rates[4]

Loan Type	Up to 36 mos. APR as low as	37-60 mos. APR as low as	61-72 mos. APR as low as	73-84 mos. APR as low as	85-96 mos. APR as low as
New Vehicle	2.49%	2.89%	2.99%	5.39%	6.29%
Late Model Used Vehicle	2.99%	3.09%	4.59%	N/A	N/A
Used Vehicle	3.89%	4.29%	4.99%	N/A	N/A

Rates as of January 09, 2020 ET.

Used Vehicles: 2018 and older model years or any model year with over 30,000 miles.
Late Model Used Vehicles: Year models 2019, 2020 and 2021 with 7,500-30,000 miles.

After applying for your auto loan, you should receive a decision on the spot or within 3-5 business days. Once you have chosen the loan you want to move forward with, you can then purchase your car. Don't worry about not using the other loans that you applied for. The other loan approvals will expire within 30-60 days of no use.

What to Do If You Have a Bad Auto Loan?

If you already have an auto loan with a high interest rate, you can try to get to refinance your loan with a bank or credit union. Your auto loan refinance will depend on the loan to value (LTV) of the vehicle and your current credit score. If you are underwater with your car loan, this means that your car is worth less than the value of your loan.

```
To calculate Loan to Value (LTV),
LTV = (Loan amount / Asset Value) x 100
```

Example 3.3:

 Your auto loan balance is $10,000, but the vehicle is only worth $8,000.

LTV = $10,000 / $8,000 x 100 = 125%.

To calculate your LTV, you take your current remaining auto loan balance and divide it by the value of the car. Then multiply by 100 to get the percentage. You will need to find out if the financial institution that you are considering will refinance your loan because the LTV ratio is more than 100%. In this example, the LTV ratio is 125%.

If you are unable to find a financial institution that will allow you to refinance your loan, you will need to pay down your loan at a more aggressive rate to get your loan balance down to or close to the value of the car. Typically, once you have done this, the bank or credit union will move forward with the refinance if your credit scores meet their threshold.

Example 3.4:

Let's use the same scenario from Example 3.3. Only this time, you want to buy another car and trade-in your current car. To buy your new car, you would have to roll $2,000 of negative equity from your old car into your new car loan ($8,000 - $10,000 = -$2,000).

I suggest that you never roll negative equity into a loan. In all honesty, you most likely can't afford these vehicles, and you are going to end up underwater on your next vehicle as well.

How to Avoid Purchasing a Car You Can't Afford

The best way to avoid these situations we recently discussed is to purchase vehicles that you can afford. A general rule of thumb is to not buy a car that costs more than 35% of your yearly income. If you cannot meet this general rule, it is okay, but don't spend too much more over 35% of your income.

Used cars under $12,000 are the sweet spot. For commuting, I prefer used cars that are 3 - 5 years old and around the $8,000 - $12,000 range. When purchasing a used car, you want to make sure that you are buying from either a reputable dealer. If you are buying a privately sold vehicle, it is a good idea to take a mechanic with you. Be sure to calculate how many miles a year, on average, the care has been driven. Anything less than twelve thousand miles per year is good. Also, ask about the maintenance history and any accidents that the vehicle has been in. Try to get the CarFax as well, if it is available.

* * *

Predatory Lending

There are places that you want to avoid because they are financial traps. These places are "Buy Here Pay Here" dealerships, furniture rental stores, and payday loan stores. When you use the services that these places offer you are setting yourself up for financial suicide. These businesses will offer you really high rates and fees and will not have your best interest. You never want to give money to places that don't care about you because when things go wrong they will spare you no mercy and will be of no help.

Let's get into the details of each of these financial traps.

Payday Loans/Cash Advances

Payday loans are typically short-term high APR loans. Payday lLoan establishments charge you extremely high interest rates on the money that you borrow. The average payday loan APR is almost 400%[8], which is insane. The average payday loan borrower ends up paying $793 in interest on a $325 loan according to a report by the Center of Responsible Lending.[9]

I suggest you stay away from these places at all costs. If you can find other alternatives to borrow money at lower rates, you should do so. Never resort to a payday loan if you have an emergency fund established. This would be an acceptable time to access the funds in this account. Other alternatives worth looking into are getting a small loan from a family member, bank or credit union, a payday advance from your employer, or a cash advance from your credit card.

Note: Credit Card Cash Advances have a higher interest rate than your standard credit card spending interest rate. Make sure to look at your statement and indicate the cash advance APR before choosing this option.

---

[8] The Balance. (2018). *Why Payday Loans and Cash Advances Are So Bad*. [online] Available at: https://www.thebalance.com/payday-loans-and-cash-advance-businesses-960026 [Accessed 12 Jan. 2020].

[9] The Balance. (2018). *Why Payday Loans and Cash Advances Are So Bad*. [online] Available at: https://www.thebalance.com/payday-loans-and-cash-advance-businesses-960026 [Accessed 12 Jan. 2020].

Buy Here Pay Here Car Dealerships

The business model of Buy Here Pay Here (BHPH) dealerships is to sell "lemon" vehicles— vehicles that have repeated, unfixable problems— to owners knowing that it is very likely for the owner to default on the loan. This would then give the dealership the opportunity to repossess the vehicle and sell it to another person, thus profiting off of the vehicle again. This cycle is repeated as many times as possible.

These places may be attractive because they offer no money down for people with poor to fair credit. They may require you to make bi-weekly payments compared to monthly payments as you would have with a traditional auto loan. The average interest rate at BHPH dealerships is around 20%, and they might put a tracker on your vehicle for easier repossession. Basically, it just isn't worth it. I suggest that you stay away from BHPH dealerships as you now know the process of securing auto loans from the previous section.

Furniture Rental Stores

When you sign a rent-to-own contract with a furniture rental store, you are agreeing to pay much more than the furniture or electronics' retail price. If you happen to fall behind on payments, these companies have the authority to pursue criminal charges against you should you not return the items after falling behind. These places are also notorious for reporting that people have not paid off their debts, leaving bad marks on credit reports although the debts have already been settled. I would advise you to stay away from these places altogether and look for other ways to find deals on furniture.

* * *

Home Loans

Home Loan Approval Process

To obtain a pre-approval letter for a mortgage, you will want to shop around the same way as you would for an auto loan. When shopping around for loans, make sure that you take advantage of any first time home buyer programs that your state or county has available.

The home loan pre-approval process requires documentation. Be prepared and have your paperwork in order before applying for mortgage pre-approval; it will make the process much smoother. Below I have listed the documentation that is typically required for the pre-approval process:

- Proof of Employment
- Proof of Income (2 Most Recent Paystubs)
- Tax Documents (W-2 and tax returns for the past 2 years)
- Place of Residence (Mail or a utility bill with your name and address listed)
- Bank Account Statements (Last month's Bank Statements)
- Credit Report (Bank will run your credit to determine your DTI ratio)
- Gift Letters (If you received any gift payments that will be used for the down payment.)

FHA Loan

A Federal Housing Administration Loan (FHA loan) is a mortgage that is issued by an approved FHA lender and insured by the Federal Housing Administration. You are required to live in the property for 12 months and can only have one FHA loan at a time. You can purchase a single family home or a 1-4 unit small apartment building with an FHA loan. FHA loans require a lower down payment and a lower credit score compared to conventional loans. You only need to make a **down payment of 3.5%** and have a **credit score of at least 580** to qualify for an FHA loan.

Note: If you are delinquent on your federal student loans or income taxes, you will not qualify for a FHA loan.

FHA loans require you to pay an Upfront Mortgage Insurance Premium (UFMIP) and an Annual Mortgage Insurance Premium (MIP) that is charged monthly. A MIP is required to be paid for the entire life of the loan if you get a 30-year loan and typically costs between 0.45% - 1.5% of the base loan amount. The average cost today is 0.85%.

Example 3.5:

If you purchase a home for $200,000. You will make annual MIP payments of

0.85% x $200,000 = $1,700

$1,700/12 = $141.67 monthly. To calculate what your MIP monthly payment would be, take the cost of the home you are looking to buy, multiply by 0.85%, then divide that number by 12.

The only way to get rid of the MIP with a 30-year mortgage is to refinance to a conventional loan.

FHA 203k Loan

An FHA 203k loan allows you to borrow money for the home purchase and the home improvement costs. The repairs and renovations costs are rolled into the loan. If you don't have the money to renovate a home and are looking for a fixer upper, this is a good option to pursue. After completing renovations on the home, it will raise the property value.

Conventional Loan

A conventional loan is a type of home loan that is not secured by a government entity. The mortgage insurance on a conventional loan can be canceled when your loan reaches 80% LTV. If you make a 20% down payment, you don't have to pay mortgage insurance at all. To qualify for a conventional loan, you will need a credit score of at least 660, a DTI ratio between 36%-43%, and a down payment of at least 3%, but 5%-20% down payment is typical.

VA Loan

A VA loan is a mortgage loan available for veterans and eligible surviving spouses. This program was established by the United States Department of Veterans Affairs. VA loans offer up to 100% financing of the value of a home, which means there is no money required for a down payment. You do not have to be a first-time home buyer to obtain a VA loan and you can have multiple VA loans at a time. If you are an active member of the military and assigned to a new duty station, you are able to purchase another property using a VA loan.

Determining How Much House You Can Afford

To determine how much house you can afford, you will use the same process as you would for auto loans. Analyze your income and expenses then determine a monthly payment amount that is suitable for your finances and will not leave you house poor — where the majority of your money is going towards your mortgage and upkeep. Visit Calculator.net again and go to their mortgage calculator. This calculator will give you a clear breakdown of your "Total Monthly Out of Pocket" payment. Do not forget to include 0.85% for the MIP payment. Play around with the numbers to get a clear picture of how much house you can afford. Calculator.net is a great resource. If you ever need to run numbers on anything, they have a calculator for it.

* * *

House Hacking

Remember how I said you can purchase a 1-4 unit small apartment building with an FHA loan? You can use your FHA loan to start generating income from your property. A good strategy is to buy a duplex or small apartment building, and live in one unit and rent out the other units. Another strategy is to rent out the other rooms or the basement in your home for additional income. Of course, do this with caution, and screen potential tenants beforehand. In some cases, the income from your tenant(s) may cover your entire mortgage. Imagine if you were able to purchase 2-4 units with your FHA loan and live entirely for free. This will help you reach financial independence much faster because rent/mortgage payments are usually where most of your money is spent every month.

Some people may be thinking, "Well I don't want to deal with the headaches of a tenant." That is perfectly fine; you don't have to. You can hire a property manager to manage your tenant for an 8-10% monthly fee if managing a tenant is not something you are interested in. If you are looking to manage the property yourself, I suggest a company called Cozy. They will handle your tenant background screening and collect your monthly rent payments for you online. It is a very simple and straight forward process to implement Cozy, and you will spend very little time managing your tenant.

If you decide to house hack then move after 12 months, remember that you will not be able to get another FHA loan unless you refinance your first property to a conventional loan. If you don't want to refinance the property, your next property will have to be a conventional loan, so keep that in mind.

I believe that your first property should be an investment property. Your investment property will be an asset that is income producing and will set you on the path to financial freedom. If you are looking for a way to live for free or mostly free, house hacking is a good option.

* * *

4

Shaping Your Future

College the Right Way

Every day on Twitter, I see someone say, "College is a scam!". Is college a scam, or did you take out more debt than you could afford given the return on investment (ROI) for the degree you chose? Sure, there are a lot of topics that you can learn online and teach yourself, but if you keep the cost of college down, you typically will come out ahead. A lot of jobs are requiring a Bachelor's degree as a basic requirement now, so if you choose to go to college, follow these steps to do it the right way.

1. Look up the average salary of the field you are interested in
2. Look at job requirements for entry-level positions
3. Go to a community college for the first 2 years
4. Take CLEP exams to gain credits for a fraction of the cost
5. Go to an in-state college/university
6. Do not take out more loans than you can afford and try to only take out federal loans (graduating with $30,000 or less in loans is ideal)
7. Join an organization and network with people in your desired field
8. Attend career fairs on campus and major organization career fairs to obtain internships or co-ops while in school.
9. Land an internship by your Sophomore summer in your field
10. Graduate with at least a 3.0 GPA

If you follow these steps and keep down the cost of college, you will have a much higher chance of being successful. I understand college may not be for everyone, but if you go to college or are still in college implement these steps and watch how everything changes for you. If you spend four years partying, not growing your network, and perfecting your craft, then you will scam yourself out of time and money.

Trades, Bootcamps, and Certifications

If you have determined that college isn't for you, don't worry, you have other options to jump-start your career. Before deciding to do anything career-wise, have a good understanding of your personality and an idea of the type of life you want to live in the future. Having this understanding will help you choose a career that aligns with your future goals and your ideal lifestyle. I see people choose careers that don't align with their ideal life and end up miserable.

If you are the kind of person who wants a flexible schedule and has every weekend off, don't choose a career/industry that doesn't allow for flexibility or give you the weekends off. If you are the kind of person who wants to work remotely from home then you should pick a career/industry where remote work is available. DO you see where I am going with this? Next, I will discuss different avenues you may want to consider if you are not interested in going to college but want to start a career.

Trades

Trades are not a route that many people think about even though there are fields that pay well. Trade jobs require vocational schooling or training to learn a specialized skillset. Skilled trades have been growing steadily for more than 20 years. Trade jobs are usually very secure due to the established unions. It is also typically affordable to attend vocational school. I have listed some of the highest paying trade jobs below.

- Air Traffic Controller
- Construction Manager
- Licensed Practical Nurse (LPN)

- Esthetician
- Pharmacy Tech
- Elevator Mechanic
- Electrician
- Energy Management
- Massage Therapist
- Cosmetology
- Culinary
- Welder (Boilermaker)
- Commercial Truck Driver (Oil Field highest paid)
- Rotary Drill Operator
- Aircraft Mechanic
- Plumber
- HVAC Technician
- Construction Equipment Operator
- Medical Equipment Repair Technician

Bootcamps

Bootcamps are fast track schooling options that allow you to transition into tech careers quickly. Bootcamps are online or in person instructor lead classes for 6 - 18 months. They are typically offered for Software Development, Web Development, UX/UI Design, and Data Analytic careers. Before deciding on a program to pursue, make sure that you do thorough research on the success of prior graduates. Focus on the average salaries, time from graduation to a job offer, programs in place to help graduates land jobs, resume/portfolio workshops, and interview preparation that the school has available for students.

Bootcamps cost much less than college but are still priced to where most people won't be able to pay cash for the program. Expect to pay between $13,000 - $20,000 for a Bootcamp program. There are a few ways that you can pay for a Bootcamp, such as a pay-as-you-go, take out a loan, or attend for free and repay by paying a percentage of your income after you obtain a job post-graduation.

Certifications

Certifications are exams that verify that you are knowledgeable on a particular subject. There are certifications available for many subjects that allow you to get started in a new career. Certifications are most popular in IT/Tech careers, but you may be able to find certifications that align with the career that you are interested in getting in to. I am most familiar with tech certifications. If you are interested in tech, I believe that these are some of the best certifications to have as of 2020.

- Amazon Web Services (AWS) Cloud Practitioner
- SalesForce Administrator
- Project Management Professional (PMP)
- CompTIA Security+
- SCRUM Master
- ITIL
- CompTIA CASP
- Microsoft Certified Solutions Expert
- Microsoft Certified Solutions Associate
- Cisco CCNP
- CompTIA A+
- Google IT Support Professional
- AWS DevOps Engineer
- PMI Agile Certified Practitioner

Do your research to determine which certifications are best for the path you want to take to start working in a new career.

* * *

Digital Assets

Digital Assets are assets that are becoming more common although some people may not view them as assets. Digital assets are digitally stored content or an online account owned by an individual or company. These assets usually produce income either actively or passively, and sometimes a mixture of both. Digital assets are a good way for someone to start making additional income. An entire book can be written on digital assets, so I implore you to do more research on each of these topics to figure out which categories work best for you.

- **Email Lists** - Email lists can be used to have control of your following on social media. Control in the sense of, if you are ever suspended or if your account gets deleted, you will always have access to your tribe that you built. You can use this list to provide value to those who enjoy your message enough to join your email list and provide them with exclusive offers.

- **Affiliate Link Websites/Accounts** - Affiliate link websites and affiliate link accounts are websites/accounts where you are paid a referral when someone buys an item using your affiliate link. Affiliate marketing sector generates millions of dollars a year, so if you are able to create a good affiliate website/account, you will be able to make money passively. An example of an affiliate account is @FatKidDeals and @QuanBotIo on Twitter. An example of an affiliate website is when you google search "best dog toys", and you click on a website that reviews dog toys and provides links to purchase the items.

- **Shopify and Etsy Websites** - Shopify and Etsy websites can be used to sell your personal products and business products. Shopify can also be used for dropshipping products for another business.

- **Domain Names** - Domain names can be purchased then sold for more money on GoDaddy.com. This is called domain flipping.

- **Digital Content** - Digital content such as ebooks, webinars, courses, guides, app templates, website templates, resume templates, graphics, artwork, anything that you can think of that is a digital product that can be sold online.

***

Entrepreneurship

Entrepreneurship is the greatest wealth builder, but it is the riskiest. There are no guarantees in investing and definitely not in entrepreneurship, so be prepared for the lifestyle. Below is a chart that shows how wealth is made up by asset class.

FINANCIAL STARTER KIT

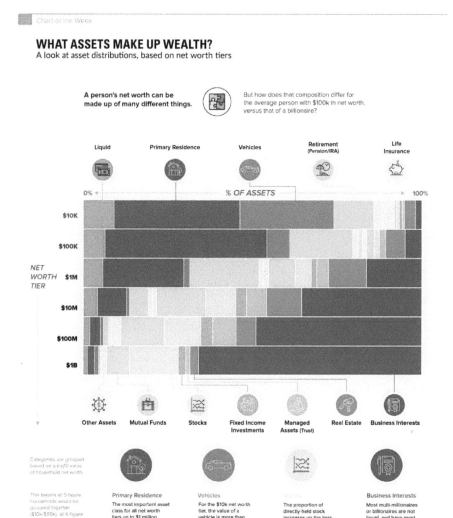

As you can see Business Interest gets larger as you go up in net worth. I often say that you do not save your way to wealth, you invest. However, the best investment made will be the one you make on yourself, whether that be learning a new skill set, investing in your business, or investing in someone else's business.

58

SHAPING YOUR FUTURE

When it comes to creating a business, you want to focus on your customer's pain points and solve their problem exceptionally well. The bigger the problem, or the more people that the problem impacts, typically, the more money you make. Everyone doesn't have to go for the big unicorn company home runs, so if you are more interested in a smaller company that is more manageable yet provides for the lifestyle you want to live, that is good too. You want to perform thorough market research before starting a new business venture.

I often hear people say that they can't wait to quit their jobs, yet some don't have much of an emergency fund or additional cash reserves. This is very risky. Something as unexpected as a trip to the emergency room can wipe you out clean, especially if you don't have any insurance after quitting your job. I recommend that people have at least 6-12 months of expenses saved before quitting their job; however, the more you have saved up, the better. The advantage of keeping your job longer is that you will have more capital to either pour into your business or invest elsewhere. Let's say you are quitting a $50,000 a year job, but you have only paid yourself $10,000 from your business. You have effectively replaced your $50,000 income with a $10,000 income and will bring more pressure onto yourself. An advantage of quitting your job is that you will have more time to put into your business. Pressure creates diamonds as they say, just be aware of the situation you are putting yourself into. It is always better to be over-prepared than unprepared.

* * *

5

The Money Mindset

You must view money as a tool that makes more money for you, provides you with your basic needs, and allows you to help others. You must understand that you are playing the long game in terms of success and wealth. You don't want to take any shortcuts along your journey to financial and personal success. Always keeping your long-term goals in mind will help you with your day-to-day decisions. When you keep your long-term goals in mind, it helps you from taking action on things that may only benefit you temporarily in the short-term but may have negative effects in the long-term.

It took me many successes and failures to realize that creating my goals and staying on my course, not getting distracted by other "shiny objects" is the best thing to do on your personal and financial journey. If you aren't familiar with shiny object syndrome, let me paint the picture. Remember a time when you decided you were going to pursue a new idea, and you started working for hours on end. Then one day, you saw another idea that became of interest to you, and you dropped your first idea altogether? That my friend is the shiny object syndrome. When you see one thing and start working on it for few weeks, then you get distracted and see another thing that you believe is better than you are already working on because it is shiny, new and seems like the best thing in the world. You end up repeating this cycle over and over again. I used to be like this, and if this is you currently, I will get into how to break this cycle later in the chapter.

I want to give you the money mindset that has led me to success. I believe these rules will reshape how you view money and lead you to success financially and life in general.

Money Mindset Rules to Live By

1. Money flows to you in abundance. There is never a lack of money or lack of opportunities.
2. Money is a tool to be used, not hoarded.
3. There is enough money to go around for everyone.
4. Never invest more than what you are willing to lose.
5. Time is worth more than money. Start looking for ways to save time. Working hard should eventually turn into working smarter and as efficiently as possible.
6. You cannot work your way to wealth, you invest your way to wealth.
7. Wealth is a long-term game.
8. Do not be afraid to lose money.
9. Do not increase expenses as your income increases.
10. View money lost as lessons learned.

Money flows to you in abundance

The law of attraction is a powerful force. When you believe that you are always open to receive money and able to create new opportunities for yourself, money will begin to flow to you naturally. Believing that there is always more money to be made will help you in the long run.

Money is a tool to be used, not hoarded

Money is to be used to provide you with your basic necessities, create more money for you, to enjoy experiences, and satisfy your wants (within reason). Once you have built your financial foundation you should use your money as a tool that you deploy to make more money for you. Think of discretionary dollars as a dollar that can go to work for you and earn money without you even lifting a finger for it.

If you only focus on saving money and never putting your money to work, you will have a large amount of cash that is sitting idle. Remember, when I talked about inflation earlier in the book? Hoarding too much money leads to idle cash that is losing value due to inflation every year.

There is enough money to go around for everyone

When you believe that there is enough money to go around for everyone you are more inclined to help other people. You never want to be greedy and not help others because you think it could hurt your chances of making money. There are a million ways to make money and the federal reserve is printing money every day. Finding opportunities for yourself and people around you will lead you to making more money in the long run.

Never invest more than what you are willing to lose

There is an old saying, "Never invest money that you can't afford to lose". This saying is true because no investment is 100% guaranteed. The moment you think you can go all in on an investment or invest money that you may need in the near future is when you will get yourself in trouble.

Time is worth more than money

Once you are financially stable, you must start valuing your time more than money. You can always create more money, but you will not ever be able to add more time. You have to start asking yourself if what you are doing is worth your time because your time is precious.

You cannot work your way to wealth, you invest your way to wealth

You create wealth by investing money that makes you more money without you having to work for it. Once you are able to remove yourself from having to trade your time for money, then you are on the right path to building wealth. Money that is creating more money for you while you are enjoying life or sleeping is the goal.

Wealth is a long-term game

Wealth is something that you strive to attain and maintain over a long period of time. You want to be able to pass down the wealth that you obtained from your hard work and smart investments to your future kids and their future kids. So, remember to always think long-term and don't make any short-term decisions that may hurt you further down the line.

Do not be afraid to lose money

When it comes to investing there is no 100% guarantee that you will always make money. You have to be okay with sometimes losing money when you put your money into an investment. The fear of losing money stops many people from investing. This is why you should never invest more than you are willing to lose. Start out small to learn how to invest, then you can gradually increase your investment size over time as you become more comfortable.

Do not increase expenses as your income increases

One of the top wealth killers is living outside of your means and increasing your spending as your income increases. Naturally, we like to treat ourselves when we get a raise. We tell ourselves, "Now I have an extra *insert amount* dollars to spend every paycheck". When we should be telling ourselves, "Now I have an additional *insert amount* to save/invest every paycheck". You must resist increasing your lifestyle/expenses as your income increases, or else you will remain in the same spot financially.

View money lost as lessons learned

You will sometimes lose money on investments/entrepreneurial ventures. Do not dwell over these losses. Regroup and review what went wrong in your investment/venture. Make a note of the mistakes and learn from the mistakes made. Do not get discouraged after a "failed" investment or venture. Elbert Hubbard once said, *"There is no failure except in no longer trying"*.

Breaking The Shiny Object Syndrome

I notice a lot of people jumping from one lane to another, which ends up slowing down their progress. For a few weeks, they are going "all in" on wholesaling, then next week they are interested in becoming a software developer, week after that it's cybersecurity, shortly after *insert skill set that is trending on social media*...you see where I am going with this? Jumping on new trends and changing directions just to end up in the same spot you were in when you first started.

This is similar to someone who is playing basketball and just pivots with no purpose spinning around and around in a circle holding the ball as the clock winds down. You aren't pivoting to help find a better angle to reach your goal, you are pivoting and wasting time.

One of my favorite entrepreneurs, Sam Ovens has a diagram that he created that shows what happens when you spread your energy out across many different things, and when you focus on one project for a long time. The diagrams look something like this.

Focused on Multiple Projects/Tasks

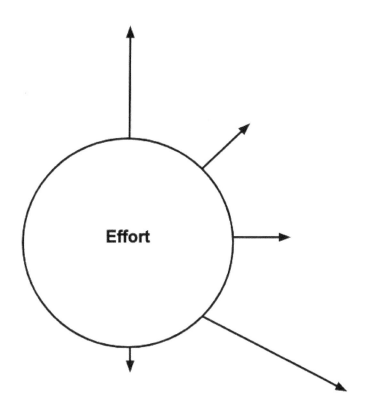

Focused on One Project/Task

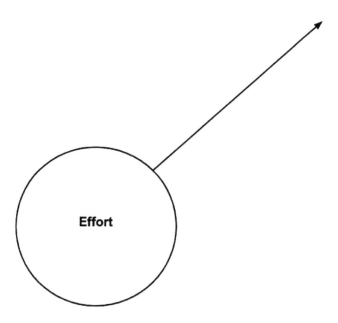

It is completely fine to be curious and not know exactly what you want to pursue next, but it is clear that a high amount of pivoting causes you to not make any progress. To break the shiny object syndrome, there are a few things that you should do before starting something new:

1. Determine if it aligns with your long-term goals.
2. Determine if it fits your personality. Research what the day-to-day of the new skill/venture looks like. Imagine yourself living that life.
3. Do research on the skill set/venture. Identify the pros and cons, different ways you can utilize the skill, projected growth/demand of the skill/industry, the average expected income after acquiring, then applying the skill and ideally how long it will take for you to see real progress in this new lane/venture.

Too many people waste time pursuing things that do not align with their long-term goals. Most of the time, short-sighted plans are a complete waste of time. Make sure your skills build upon each other like building blocks to strengthen your arsenal. Even when it comes down to business, you want to make sure that you are learning new skills that help you grow your business or create new revenue streams for your business. This is called vertical integration and it can be applied to everything in life.

So, you might be wondering, "How do I go about conducting this research?". Some options for you:

- Use Google to find articles related to the growth/outlook of an industry
- Use YouTube to find videos discussing the day in the life of a/an *insert title*
- Use YouTube to find videos discussing the pros and cons of a skillset/investment
- Find people who are where you want to be and talk to them. You can use Twitter, Instagram, or go out and network in person. Yes, I said in person.
- Read books and listen to podcasts based on the skillset/field

I want people to pivot with a purpose when choosing different skills or investment vehicles and stop spinning around in circles as time passes them by. Spend time researching what you want to do before you actually decide to pursue it. This will save you a ton of time and headaches in the long run.

* * *

6

Retirement

Retirement Accounts

This chapter will explain the different kinds of retirement accounts, how they are used, and their advantages and disadvantages. It is good to incorporate retirement accounts into your long-term financial plans due to their tax advantages and free money that you can get from your employer's 401(k) matching. It's all about building a well-rounded financial portfolio.

Traditional 401(k)

A traditional 401(k) plan is a company sponsored retirement account that employees can contribute to. Employers may also make a matching contribution. The money that you contribute to your 401(k) lowers your taxable income. When contributing money to a traditional 401(k), the money will not be taxed until you withdraw it from the account. You will be taxed at whatever your tax rate is at the time of withdrawal. There are limits to how much you can contribute to your 401(k) plan. These limits are determined by the Internal Revenue Service (IRS).

RETIREMENT

As of 2020 here are the 401(k) contribution limits

Type of Contribution	2019 Tax Year	2020 Tax Year
Elective deferrals	$19,000	$19,500
Catch-up contributions	$6,000	$6,500
Total elective deferral limit (50 or older)	$25,000	$26,000
Overall contribution limit (under 50)	$56,000	$57,000
Overall contribution limit (50 or older)	$62,000	$63,500

DATA SOURCE: IRS.

Loophole: There is a tax loophole to get around the max contributions to a 401(k) plan, which is called the "Mega Backdoor Roth". This allows you to contribute an additional $37,500 into a Roth IRA.

Employers may offer a match on your contributions to your 401(k) plan. This is called 401(k) matching. The match amount depends on the employer. To see what your employer offers, take a look at your benefits package. Some common matches that employers offer: 3% of your total salary match and 50 cents or a dollar for every dollar you contribute up to a certain percentage of your salary.

Example 6.1:

An employee contributes 3% to meet their employers' 3% match limit. If your salary is $10,000 and you contribute $300 (3% of your total salary), your employer will match and put an additional $300 in your 401(k) account. At the end of the year, you will have acquired a total of $600 in your 401(k), although you only contributed $300. This is effectively a 100% return.

You want to take full advantage of your employers' match if they offer it. It is free money, who doesn't like FREE money? At the bare minimum, you want to meet your employer's match.

When contributing to your 401(k), you will be responsible for choosing specific investments. These investments are typically stocks, bonds, index funds, and target-date funds. You will specify how you want to allocate your contributions to the available investments by choosing a percentage you want to allocate to each offering. The percentage must add up to 100%. I suggest you take a look at the investment options your company has available in your 401(k) plan because all company offerings differ. Do research on each of the offerings on Morningstar.com.

Roth 401(k)

A Roth 401(k) plan allows you to contribute to the account and pay taxes upfront, allowing the money to grow tax-free. When you withdraw from a Roth 401(k), you will not pay any taxes. People find these plans to be advantageous because they predict to be in a higher tax bracket at the time of retirement. In this case, they want to pay lower taxes at the beginning of their career to avoid paying higher taxes in the future. There are income limits for Roth accounts that I have shown below.

Loophole: If you are above these limits there is a tax loophole that you can take advantage of called the "Backdoor Roth", which allows you to still contribute to a Roth account even if your income is higher.

Withdrawing From a 401(k) Plan

One of the major disadvantages of 401(k) plans is that it is hard to withdraw the money from the account without penalty. To withdraw from your

401(k) account without penalty you must be at least age 59 $^{1/2}$ or meet other criteria set by the IRS. Visit the IRS.gov website to become familiar with the laws for withdrawing from 401(k) plans. You can also withdraw money from your 401(k) by taking a loan on the account, but make sure to do your research first. Remember, this is a long-term retirement account, and your goal is to grow your money over a long period of time, so think long and hard about withdrawing from this account.

If you leave a job, you can rollover your 401(k) balance into an IRA of your choice (Vanguard and Fidelity are good options) or into your new employer's 401(k) and avoid withdrawal fees. Be sure to follow the rules that the IRS has established for rolling over your 401(k) to not face any penalties. It's a fairly simple process, but you want to do your research before performing the rollover.

Traditional Individual Retirement Account (IRA)

A traditional Individual Retirement Account (IRA) is a tax-advantaged investment account that an individual can use to save funds for retirement. IRA accounts lower your taxable income in a similar fashion to 401(k) accounts. The IRA contribution limit is $6,000 or your total earned income for the year, whichever is lower. The advantage of IRA's is that you do not rely on an employer for access, and you have more investment options based on the brokerage that you decide to open an account with. You will have a full range of investment selection with your IRA including stocks, bonds, ETFs, and mutual funds compared to only having a set selection chosen by your employer available to invest in a 401(k).

There are contribution limits and income phaseout ranges for deducting IRA contributions if you have a retirement plan.

If you have a retirement plan at work, your ability to take the traditional IRA deduction is subject to these income limitations for 2020:

Tax Filing Status	2020 Traditional IRA Full Deduction AGI Limit	Phase-Out Limit
Single or head of household	$65,000	$75,000
Married filing jointly	$104,000	$124,000
Married filing separately	$0	$10,000

DATA SOURCE: IRS. AGI = ADJUSTED GROSS INCOME.

If you don't have an employer's retirement plan at work, but your spouse does, your ability to use the traditional IRA deduction is limited, as shown below:

Tax Filing Status	2020 Traditional IRA Full Deduction AGI Limit	Phase-Out Limit
Married filing jointly	$196,000	$206,000
Married filing separately	$0	$10,000

DATA SOURCE: IRS.

An IRA can only be funded with earned income. Income from investments, Social Security benefits, or child support does not count as earned income. Since an IRA is another type of retirement account, you will face a 10% withdrawal fee for withdrawals before age 59 1/2. You also have to pay income tax on your early withdrawal from a traditional IRA. Starting at age 70 1/2, holders of traditional IRAs must begin taking required minimum distributions (RMDs). After RMDs begin, you can no longer contribute to a traditional IRA.

Roth IRA

A Roth IRA is similar to a traditional IRA, but Roth IRA contributions are not tax-deductible, and qualified distributions are tax-free. You contribute to a Roth IRA using after-tax dollars, but you do not pay any taxes on investment gains. When you reach retirement age, you can withdraw from the account without incurring any income taxes on your withdrawals. Unlike traditional IRAs, you are able to contribute to a Roth IRA as long as you have eligible earned income, no matter how old you are.

Roth IRA income limitations and maximum contribution limits are shown below:

Tax Filing Status	2020 Roth IRA Full Contribution AGI Limit	Phase-Out Limit
Single or head of household	$124,000	$139,000
Married filing jointly	$196,000	$206,000
Married filing separately	$0	$10,000

DATA SOURCE: IRS.

Simplified Employee Pension IRA (SEP IRA)

A Simplified Employee Pension (SEP) IRA is a type of traditional IRA for self-employed individuals or small business owners. Any business owner with one or more employees or anyone with freelance income can open a SEP-IRA. Contributions into a SEP-IRA are tax-deductible, and you are allowed to invest your money in many ways. The biggest advantage of SEP-IRAs is that you can invest your money into other investments, such as real estate. If you are a business owner, I highly suggest you take a further look into SEP IRAs.

* * *

FIRE

I learned about Financial Independence Retire Early (FIRE) in 2014, and it is what got me hooked on personal finance. I went down a long rabbit hole of articles on Mr. Money Mustache's websites for hours a day. FIRE is an early retirement method of saving as much of your income as possible to invest and keeping expenses as low as possible to reach financial independence at an early age. Financial independence is when your passive income is able to cover all of your living expenses.

There are different varieties of FIRE. There's a very extreme frugal approach where the aim is to save/invest 80+% of income. Then there's the extreme approach where the aim is to save/invest between 50% - 80% of income. Lastly, there's the moderately frugal approach where the aim is to save/invest 30% - 40% of income and use other investments to speed up the early retirement process.

I am not a fan of extreme frugality because I believe that people shouldn't focus so much on cutting everything they enjoy out of their lives. It's okay to make temporary cuts, but permanently cutting something from your life for the sake of early retirement just isn't something that I can get down with. I suggest that you look to increase income before you decide to start cutting out things that you enjoy. If a $5 Starbucks coffee is stopping you from early retirement, you need to figure out how to make an extra $5 a day.

Below is a chart from Mr. Money Mustache's blog that shows how your savings rate correlates to retirement.

Savings Rate (Percent)	Working Years Until Retirement
5	66
10	51
15	43
20	37
25	32
30	28
35	25
40	22
45	19
50	17
55	14.5
60	12.5
65	10.5
70	8.5
75	7
80	5.5
85	4
90	Under 3
95	Under 2
100	Zero

People aim to FIRE by investing their income in an index fund that pays out dividends or tracks the S&P 500. They plan on funding their retirement account until they reach their target retirement number. This target retirement number is calculated by calculating their yearly expenses and multiplying that number by 25.

```
Target FIRE Number = Yearly Expenses x 25
```

Once they reach their FIRE number, they will safely withdraw 4% of their account a year. So, for every $1,000,000 in a retirement account, you can safely withdraw $40,000. The younger you plan on retiring, the lower your safe withdrawal rate should be. I would be as cautious and prepared as possible when following this methodology, and I would recommend you use a safe withdrawal rate of 3% instead of 4%. So, for every $1,000,000 in a retirement account, you can safely withdraw $30,000, and your target FIRE number would be Yearly Expenses x 33.3.

```
Conservative Target FIRE Number = Yearly Expenses x 33.3
```

There are many people that have joined the FIRE movement. If it is something that interests you, I suggest you do more research on blogs, Twitter, and YouTube, and find a tribe that can give you tips throughout your FIRE journey.

* * *

How to Retire With A Million Dollars

Now that you have learned about 401(k) and IRA accounts, I want to break down the math behind retiring with a million dollars. When it comes to investing, time is always on your side. The earlier you start consistently investing and the more time you have until retirement, the easier it is to retire with a million dollars. You can still retire with a million dollars if you start later on in life, but you will have to invest more money. I will show you how to retire with a million dollars at all walks of life, 15-year, 20-year, 30-year, and 40-year time frames.

20 Years Until Retirement

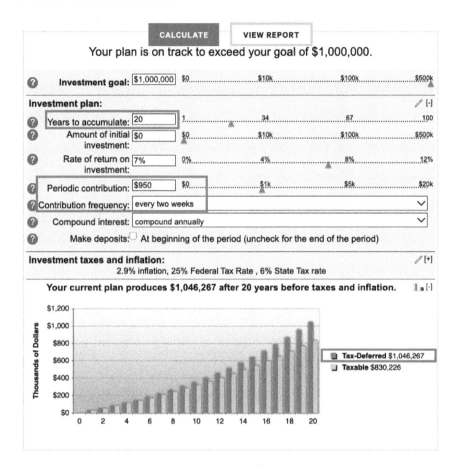

You need to invest $950 every two weeks into a traditional retirement account with a 7% return rate compounded annually for 20 years to retire with a million dollars.

25 Years Until Retirement

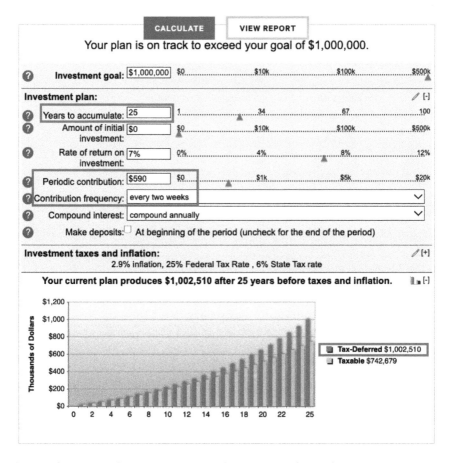

You need to invest $590 every two weeks into a traditional retirement account with a 7% return rate compounded annually for 25 years to retire with a million dollars.

RETIREMENT

30 Years Until Retirement

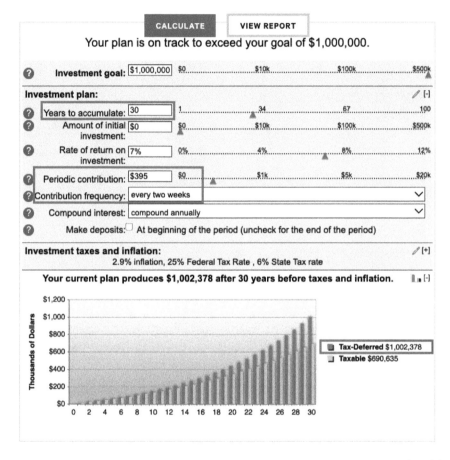

You need to invest $395 every two weeks into a traditional retirement/401(k) account with a 7% return rate compounded annually for 30 years to retire with a million dollars.

40 Years Until Retirement

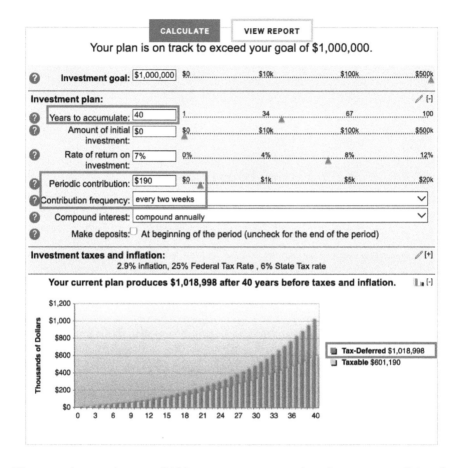

You need to invest $190 every two weeks into a traditional retirement/401(k)account with a 7% return rate compounded annually for 40 years to retire with a million dollars.

RETIREMENT

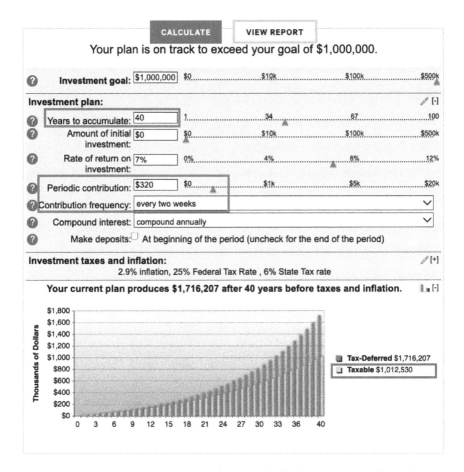

You need to invest $320 every two weeks into a Roth IRA account with a 7% return rate compounded annually for 40 years to retire with a million dollars. NOTE: Roth IRA's current limit is $6,000 a year if you are under the age of 50

As you can see the more time you have until retirement, the less money that you need to invest. If you are interested in running your own numbers, you can go to BankRate's investment calculator (www.bankrate.com/calculators/retirement/investment-goal-calculator). Time works in your favor due to compounding interest. *Compound interest* is the interest that you earn on interest. In other words, when you reinvest the money made from your initial investment back into the same investment, you are generating compounded interest.

FINANCIAL STARTER KIT

Example 6.2: You invest $100 into an investment that will give you a 10% return in 1 month. After a month has passed, you receive your initial $100 investment plus the 10% return ($10), which now gives you a total of $110. You decide that you want to reinvest the full $110 into the same investment to gain another 10% return.

After another month passes, you now receive your initial $110 investment plus the 10% return ($11), which gives you a total of $121. In two months, your initial $100 has given you a return of $10 the first month and $11 the second month. This is the power of compound interest at work.

* * *

7

Outro

I wrote this book to help people gain financial literacy quickly. I remember when I started my financial literacy journey when I was only 19. I am now 27. This journey has been one of trial and error; however, I made up my mind about fixing my financial situation and was able to reach financial freedom at the end of 2019. My investments now cover all of my expenses. I wish for everyone to be able to reach this point in life, should it be something they aspire for themselves. I wrote this book to serve as a guide that people can revisit when they are about to make a financial decision, and avoid all of the hard lessons that I had to learn through trial and error.

Everyone's journey is different, but the foundation is the same. Without a solid foundation, you will fall victim to all of the traps that they set out for you. They want you to be another average statistic. I'm here to tell you that everyone has the ability to become financially free by making smart financial decisions and avoiding the traps of the American Dream.

After reading this book, take a real look at your finances, place your assets and liabilities in Personal Capital to view and track your net worth, and create a Mint account to track your spending. Make a plan to improve your financial situation and stick to it.

* * *

If you are interested in a free M1 Investing Guide, you can gain free access at M1Guide.CapitalSb.com

If you are interested in a one-on-one consultation call for Financial Revamps, Career Planning (IT/Tech/Engineering/Defense Industry), and Overseas Contractor Blueprints, they are available on my website BookWithBeez.com.

If you are interested in learning more about my Defense Industry Guide, you can learn more at www.DefenseIndustry.guide.

Thank you for taking the time to read this book. If you enjoyed it use the hashtag #FinancialStarterKit and let me know how it helped you on Twitter @capital_sb and tag me on Instagram @capital.sb.

Resources

- Monthly Allocation Spreadsheet (Go to allocate.capitalsb.com to download it for free)
- My free M1 Investing Guide, store.capitalsb.com/m1. Get a free $10 and start investing on M1 m1.capitalsb.com
- AnnualCreditReport.com for free annual credit report
- Mint.com - Free budgeting website
- Personal Capital - pc.Capitalsb.com. Get a free $20 and start tracking your net worth
- Discover Credit Card Referral discover.capitalsb.com. Receive a $50 $50 statement credit (make sure you select to secured or unsecured before applying)
- CreditKarma.com - Free credit score checks to monitor your credit
- Calculator.net - Website to calculate investment returns
- Bankrate.com - Website to calculate investment returns
- Morningstar.com - Website to research stocks
- Cozy.com - Free rental property management software

I want to give you some other books that were extremely helpful in my financial literacy journey as well.

OUTRO

- The Richest Man in Babylon by George S. Clason
- Unscripted by MJ DeMarco
- Rich Dad Poor Dad by Robert Kiyosaki
- The E-Myth Revisited by Michael E Gerber
- Family Wealth Keeping It in the Family by Hughes Jr E
- Think and Grow Rich by Napoleon Hill
- The Simple Path to Wealth by JL Collins
- The Millionaire Real Estate Investor
- Profit First by Mike Michalowicz
- The One Thing by Gary W. Keller and Jay Papasan

* * *

Financial Starter Kit Checklist
Congratulations on finishing the Financial Starter Kit!

Complete the Financial Starter Kit checklist to start your financial journey.

FINANCIAL
STARTER KIT
CHECKLIST

Now that you have completed the book, work your way through this checklist to take control of your finances.

FINANCIAL OVERVIEW
- ☐ Complete your financial overview
  - ☐ Calculate your total monthly income
  - ☐ Calculate your total monthly expenses
  - ☐ Calculate your remaining discretionary income (Income - Expenses). Refer to Chapter 2: Creating a Solid Foundation, Section: How to Determine Your Allocations
  - ☐ Calculate your total credit card debt and monthly payments
  - ☐ Calculate your remaining student loan debt
  - ☐ Calculate your total personal debts
  - ☐ Make a savings plan, debt paydown plan, or investing plan
- ☐ Download the Money Allocation Spreadsheet and create your allocations
- ☐ Download your bank statements to view the fees charged last month by the bank
- ☐ Open an account with a bank or credit union that does not charge fees. Set up checkings and savings accounts as needed
- ☐ Open a High Yield Savings account for your Emergency Fund (Ally , Barclays, Marcus, Discover, Wealthfront or American Express)
- ☐ Create a Mint (www.mint.com) account, then link your bank accounts and credit cards to monitor your spending
- ☐ Create a Personal Capital (www.personalcapital.com) account, then link your bank accounts, credit cards, loans, retirement accounts, and car to view your net worth

CREDIT
- ☐ Request your Credit Report (www.annualcreditreport.com) from all three credit bureaus (Experian, Transunion, and Equifax)
- ☐ Create a Credit Karma (www.creditkarma.com) account to monitor your credit score
- ☐ Look to see if any of your current financial institutions or credit cards offer free FICO scores

CAR
- ☐ Look up the current value of your car (www.kbb.com)
- ☐ Find your current remaining balance of the auto loan
- ☐ Find your current APR and length of the loan. Look into refinancing your loan if you have unfavorable loan terms

LIFE INSURANCE
- ☐ Request a life insurance quote online if you do not have life insurance and sign up for a plan

RETIREMENT
- ☐ Review your company's benefits plan to find out the 401K matching details. Also make note of when the money is vested
- ☐ View your company's 401K stock offerings. Look up these offerings on Morningstar.com
- ☐ Set up your 401K to contribute at least up to the match

NOTES

FINANCIAL STARTER KIT

NOTES

FINANCIAL STARTER KIT

NOTES

FINANCIAL STARTER KIT

CPSIA information can be obtained
at www.ICGtesting.com
Printed in the USA
LVHW070225301220
675352LV00022B/551